SECOND EDITION

COMPLETE PUMPING NYLON

The Classical Guitarist's Technique Handbook

SCOTT TENNANT

CONTENTS

*"Composer, sculptor, painter, poet, prophet, sage,
these are the makers of the after-world,
the architects of heaven.
The world is beautiful because they have lived;
without them, laboring humanity would perish."*

—James Allen
(from: *As a Man Thinketh*)

for Joe Fava
1911 — 1994
teacher and friend

Alfred Music
P.O. Box 10003
Van Nuys, CA 91410-0003
alfred.com

ISBN-10: 1-4706-3517-8
(Book & Online Video/Audio)

ISBN-13: 978-1-4706-3517-6
(Book & Online Video/Audio)

Illustrations: Barbara Smolover
Cover Photos: © Howard Sokol/
Tony Stone Images; Guitar on cover
by Richard Bruné

Edited by
Nathaniel Gunod

Alfred Cares. Contents printed on
environmentally responsible paper.

SCOTT TENNANT

Considered one of the world's premiere guitar virtuosos, Scott Tennant is a founding member of the Grammy Award-winning ensemble the Los Angeles Guitar Quartet (LAGQ). He concertizes worldwide and has recorded as a soloist with the recording labels Guitar Co-op, GHA, and Delos. With the LAGQ, Scott has recorded with the labels GHA, Delos, Sony Classical, Windham Hill, Deutsche Grammophon, and Telarc. The LAGQ's Telarc release *LAGQ: Latin* was nominated for a Grammy, while *LAGQ'S Guitar Heroes* (Telarc) won the 2005 Grammy for Best Classical Crossover Album.

Whenever time allows, Scott is an avid collector of all things "tech" and "gears"—including bikes, watches, clocks, and old cell phones. He also takes his coffee brewing and roasting skills very seriously. Scott's two favorite nonmusical achievements are being invited to participate in a Wing Chun demonstration with sifu Alan Lamb and students at the 2005 Bruce Lee convention in Los Angeles, and being named the Customer of the Week for a record-setting three times at his local Peet's Coffee establishment.

Scott devotes most of his time to teaching guitar and performance practice in master classes and residencies, in addition to his renowned *Pumping Nylon* workshops. His book *Pumping Nylon* has inspired and guided countless guitar students, enthusiasts, and professionals since its release in 1995, and it continues to be a best-seller in over 20 countries. Scott has been on the faculty of the San Francisco Conservatory and the Pasadena Conservatory of Music, and currently lives in Los Angeles, CA, where he is a professor of guitar studies at the USC Thornton School of Music.

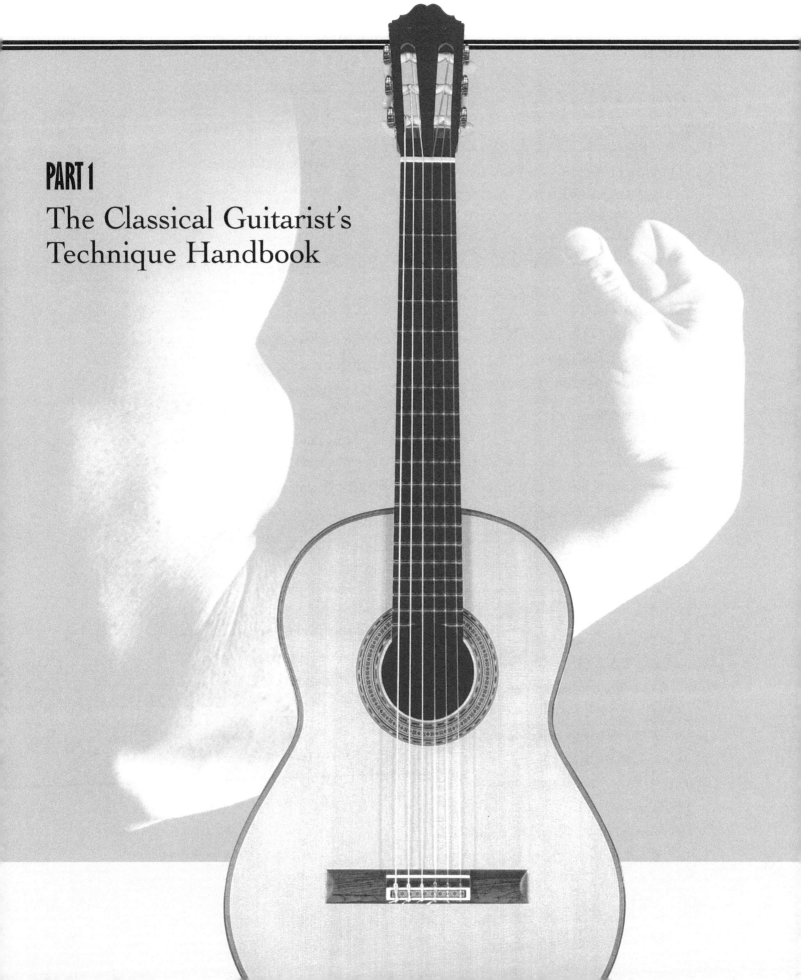

SECOND EDITION

COMPLETE PUMPING NYLON

PART 1

The Classical Guitarist's
Technique Handbook

CONTENTS

AUTHOR'S PREFACE

Welcome to the second edition of *Pumping Nylon*, or as I like to call it: the PN 2.0 upgrade!

My goals for *Pumping Nylon* have always been to offer ideas to help dissolve some of our most stubborn technical knots and to clarify a number of issues we all have in playing classical guitar. I say "we" because I am a lifetime student myself, and I learn just as much, or more, from teaching as I did from taking lessons or playing in master classes. I am in this with you. In fact, everything I share in this book comes from material and concepts I've used myself over the years, so I know they work. I'm not saying, nor will I ever say, that this is the only way or best way. But it is the way that helped me.

Please don't confuse this book with a method book. *Pumping Nylon* is not sequenced progressively, as a method would be, but it is, instead, conveniently divided into "Left Hand" and "Right Hand" sections. It is more of a reference book or technique manual.

The pieces presented in this edition are wonderful and tempting. Try them! Each composition comes with its own set of details and tips. If you find that they are way over your head, keep your chin up and use the technical instruction to sharpen your current repertoire. As always, I encourage you to invent your own exercises whenever necessary, especially since all of our technical needs are so different.

I cannot begin to express how much I have enjoyed creating this second edition for you. The core material remains, but we added new instructional text, advice, studies, and compositions. I hope this "upgrade" will help bump your skills up to a new level. Now get plucking!

I want to extend special thanks to...

Brian Head, Andy York, and Evan Hirschelman for composing their wonderful "made-to-order" etudes; Ines Thomé, Mak Grgic, Cameron O'Connor, and Noah Kim for appearing on the video; Billy Arcila for posing for the photos from which the illustrations were rendered; Durmel DeLeon for the photography; John Dearman, Matt Greif, Bill Kanengiser, and Mark Simons for their technical assistance and pedagogical advice; Nat Gunod, my friend and editor, for his guidance and patience; my students who were (not always voluntary) "guinea pigs" for much of the material contained herein; my many friends and colleagues who have continually used this book in their teaching; and you who are now reading this for your support.

EDITOR'S PREFACE

It's hard to believe that 20 years have gone by since we released the first edition of *Pumping Nylon*. Scott Tennant did an amazing job writing this book the first time around. In the ensuing years, he has developed many of his ideas further and has become an even better teacher.

This second edition is a definite upgrade of the original. The wealth of technical information—still not readily available elsewhere—is supplemented by a variety of both well- and lesser-known technical exercises, such as the *120 Right-Hand Studies* of Mauro Giuliani and arpeggio studies by Francesco Tarrega that were included in the first edition. In this second edition, we have also included Giuliani's *Left-Hand Etudes, Op. 1*, invaluable exercises for developing left-hand technique. The original four studies composed especially for *Pumping Nylon*, two by Brian Head and two by Andrew York, are still included but are now accompanied by three wonderful new etudes (*Movements I and II* from "May the Notes Be With You" and *Shapeshifting*) by Evan Hirschelman. All seven of these *Pumping Nylon* etudes are concert-worthy repertoire.

The music engravings in the second edition have been improved for better readability. Notice, especially, that the Giuliani *120 Right-Hand Studies* are now offered at full size, making them much easier to read. Plus, but we have added pages (the original 96-page book has grown to 144!) and premium comb binding to improve usability.

Pumping Nylon is keeping up with the times. In addition to making a new, improved edition of the book, we have put together an entirely new *Pumping Nylon* video, which is available online to either stream or download. The video includes masterful performances by guitarists Ines Thomé, Mak Grgic, Cameron O'Connor, Evan Hirschelman, and Scott Tennant himself playing Brian Head's challenging tremolo piece, *Chant*. And to say video technology has improved since the mid 1990s is an understatement. The new video looks terrific.

As I stated in the preface to the first edition, anyone who has studied classical guitar is going to find something in this book that directly contradicts what you have been taught—or what you teach. This is inevitable. If you dismiss this work for that reason, you will be missing much. Read on. Take a look at all the ideas presented here by this great player and teacher. You will come away better for it.

You should also check out Scott Tennant's edition of "Recuerdos de la Alhambra" by Tárrega. It includes even more lessons and exercises for the development of tremolo.

It has become commonplace to find well-worn copies of this book in students' hands. The acceptance of this work into the classical guitar vernacular has been very rewarding. We felt we owed it to our community of teachers and students to make this edition of the book even better. We are deeply grateful for the input and support *Pumping Nylon* has received. If you have the first edition, it's time for an upgrade!

Nathaniel Gunod
October 2015

Track 1

MP3 audio is included with this book to make learning easier and more enjoyable. The symbol shown on the left appears next to every example in the book that features an MP3 track. Use the MP3s to ensure you're capturing the feel of the examples and interpreting the rhythms correctly. The track number below the symbol corresponds directly to the example you want to hear.

To access the MP3s, see the insert card attached to the inside back cover of the book.

Track 1 is a tuning track you can use to make sure your guitar is tuned the same as the guitar in the recording.

SOME DO'S AND DON'TS

About the Hands

Before we immerse ourselves in the technical exercises in this book, let's cover some basics. There are numerous guitarists who, despite the seemingly awkward appearance of their hands, posture, and technique, produce amazing results. Generally, the philosophy is to leave well-enough alone (or, "if it ain't broke, don't fix it"). My original intention for this book was to avoid telling people exactly how to hold their hands, how to sit, etc. But there are some physical problems which one should avoid, and some basic truths that need to be addressed.

The hands should be in a constant state of *dynamic relaxation*. This means they should always be free of excess tension. At the same time, they should always be on stand-by; ready to play in an instant. Then they should empty, or relax, just as quickly. In order for all of this to happen, the hands need to be positioned as naturally as is possible while maintaining an advantageous angle to the strings.

For maximum results, the wrists of both the hands should be naturally straight (in relation to the arm), not forced into being straight. The diagrams below illustrate this point.

See here how the wrist is straight on the top-side of the hand, and not on the bottom-side.

Here the wrist is bent too much, and thus not allowing the tendons to work easily.

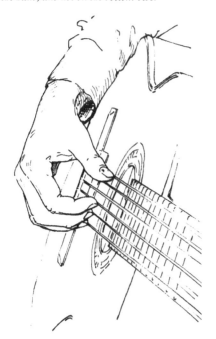 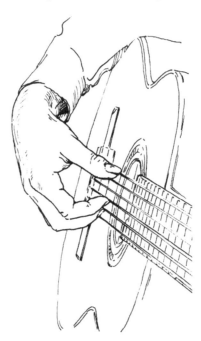

Try this experiment: keeping your wrist bent, make a fist. Not very comfortable, is it? In order for the fingers to work correctly, comfortably, and for extended periods of time, the tendons must be as free as possible to move around (like the cables that they are) inside the carpal tunnel. The carpal tunnel is the boney passage in your wrist. Bending the wrist too far aggravates the tendons, and could eventually cause irreparable damage.

In the two diagrams that follow, notice how the same principle applies to the left hand.

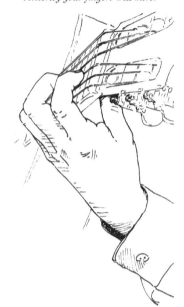

The straighter the wrist, the more dexterity your fingers will have.

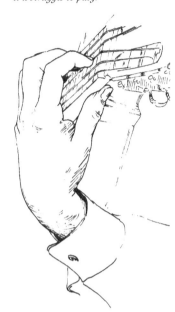

Bending your wrist too much makes it a struggle to play.

As for your left-hand thumb, it's generally wise to keep it positioned just under your second (middle) finger. This creates somewhat of a vise, and allows for an even distribution of pressure throughout the hand.

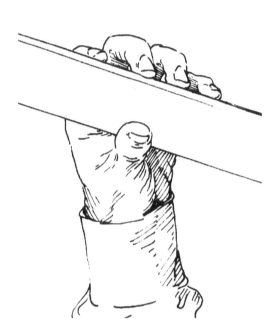

About the Body

The body should also be in a relaxed state. While seated, try stretching your neck and spine upwards towards the ceiling, pulling your shoulders back slightly (just enough to keep them from drooping forward). Now, relax your muscles so that your body sort of freezes itself in that position. This is a good state for the body to settle into. Your shoulders should not crunch upward into your neck. Take a look at the illustrations in the following section about holding the guitar.

About Holding the Guitar
—The Triangle

The guitar touches the body at three points to create a triangle:
1. At the lower part of the chest (near the sternum).
2. At the top of the left thigh.
3. At the inner part of the right thigh.

Of course, the reverse applies if you play left-handed! This triangle is held into place when the right forearm is rested on the instrument.

It's basic, yes, but this position provides the best angle for the guitar. For good tone production, especially in a concert situation, it is essential that the vibration of the back of the guitar is not compromised by placing it flat against your stomach. Since the guitar is such a directional instrument (it sounds best wherever you aim the soundhole), this angle also allows for the sound to travel a greater distance, because it keeps us from pointing the instrument at the floor. Most importantly, this angle helps keep the arms and hands in more advantageous positions for playing.

Footstool Alternatives

There are many alternatives to the footstool for keeping your guitar up at an angle. These come in the form of various devices that either attach to your guitar, or rest on your leg, and they allow you to keep both your feet flat on the floor. They are widely available at many retailers around the world. If you are experiencing any discomfort in your back, knees, legs, arms, or shoulders, I encourage you to experiment with them to see if they relieve the awkwardness. Like so many other guitarists, you may find you prefer them to a footstool.

Dynarette Cushion

ErgoPlay

"Failure to prepare is preparing to fail."

• John Wooden, former UCLA basketball coach •

THE LEFT HAND

Finger Placement and Accuracy

It is vital that one adopt a strong left-hand "stance" and place the fingers in a position which allows for maximum reach and flexibility.

As you can see from the illustration below, the fingers of the left hand are not all placed on the center of the fingertips. Rather, an advantageous position for the left hand is as follows:

1. The first finger (1) plays on the left side of its tip.
2. The second finger (2) plays just to the left of its tip.
3. The third finger (3) plays just to the right of its tip.
4. The fourth finger (4) makes contact on the right side of its tip.

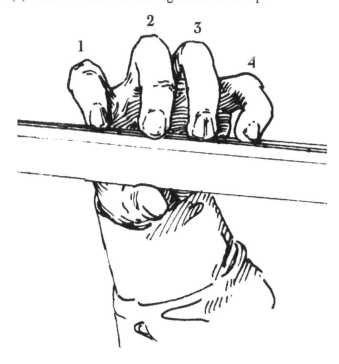

This position brings the larger muscles on either side of the hand into play, not necessarily to support fingers 1 and 4 (although this is a benefit), but to balance the whole hand and give it a stronger, more secure stance. It also allows for greater finger dexterity.

Notice the space between the middle joints of each finger. They're not touching! Not only are they not touching, but there is an intentional amount of extra space. This allows the fingers to spread apart and reach with greater speed when necessary. Never allow these joints to touch. This actually takes more muscular effort than keeping them apart, and the buzzword of this book is "economy": *economy of effort, economy of energy, economy of motion*.

As for the thumb, keep it just under the second finger. This helps to distribute the pressure evenly between the fingers and thumb, creating a sort of vise.

Pressure and Release

To familiarize yourself with this left-hand position, especially if it's new for you, practice the following.

Pressure/Release Exercise

Place your left hand in the correct position as shown on page 12. (Don't neglect your thumb, either.) Place fingers 1, 2, 3, and 4 on frets I, II, III, and IV respectively on any string (although I suggest you start with the third string ③). Press them down on the string and then *empty* them (release the pressure), keeping your fingers on the string. From this "relaxed-on-the-string" position, proceed to press the four fingers down, then empty them. Press, then empty. Press, then empty, and so on. Do this a number of times while keeping your fingers on the string. The point of this exercise is to feel the immediacy with which your fingers press (apply pressure), and then empty (totally release pressure) with the same immediacy. All four fingers should press and release simultaneously. Feel the vise grip we spoke of earlier. Feel the pressure distribute evenly throughout all four fingers and thumb.

After you have repeated this many times and gotten the hang of it, try it pressing the fingers down one at a time. Start from the same position as before: with all four fingers touching the string but not pressing.

Finger Exchange

As elementary as it may seem, we have just touched upon the most important issue concerning a good left hand: controlling the pressure and relaxation in the fingers. Now let's move on and approach exchanging fingers in the same manner.

The issue with exchanging fingers is maintaining the proper distance from the string. Notice in the illustration on the right that the fingers are all roughly the same distance to the string.

Ideally, the fingers should be about half an inch above the string, but definitely no more than one inch. Moving the fingers any more than one inch above the string defeats our goal of economy of movement.

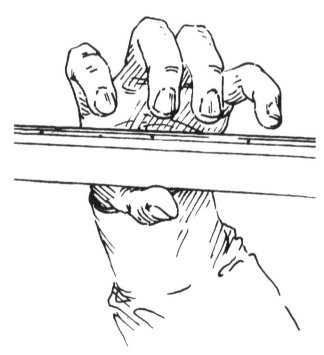

From this position, we will practice the following chromatic scale. With the same immediacy as in the previous drill, press the fingers down and empty them, one at a time, in order. This time, however, do not keep your fingers touching the string when not playing. When you empty a finger that has finished playing, spring it back into its place; about half an inch above the string. Since we will be dealing with the right hand in a later section, don't worry about which right-hand fingering to use for now. A simple *i–m* alternation will do. Use rest stroke or free stroke—it doesn't matter. Just focus on your left hand.

As one finger empties, make sure that the next *fills up* with exactly the same amount of pressure. I like to imagine this exchange as a shifting of weight from finger to finger. As you feel the weight shift, don't feel it only in the fingers, but throughout the whole hand. This will give you a heightened awareness of the balance in the hand.

Ascending Slurs (Hammer-ons)

A good, solid ascending slur, (or, as it would lazily roll off our tongues in simpler times, "hammer-on"), is nothing more than a slightly more energetic approach to the pressure/release applications.

From the half an inch hovering position pictured in the last diagram, simply snap the desired finger onto the string. If you have diligently practiced the pressure/release exercises up until now, the feeling during execution of the slur is the same. The pressure is quick and accurate. In the case of the slur, the finger must be snapped down onto the string with slightly greater speed. This is what produces the sound and creates our tone during a slur. Don't think of bringing the finger up any further above the string than half an inch to an inch, or pressing down on the string any harder. The speed is what counts. I like to use the word "snap" when referring to a slur, because, for me, that's what it feels and sounds like.

In the following simple exercise, take your time and do several repetitions of each slur.

DO: snap the finger quickly and cleanly onto the string.
DON'T: continue to apply extra pressure once you're on the string.

If your slur is quick enough, the force with which you come down onto the string will be enough to keep the note sounding clearly.

Repeat each example at least 4x.

As in the pressure/release exercises, the shifting of weight from finger to finger is a must. Just before a finger executes its slur, it is empty. As it executes the slur, it fills up (with energy), and with a combination of muscle and weight (momentum), snaps onto the string; all in the blink of an eye.

Have faith! Work speed, not force and tension, into your slurs. And before you start complaining that half an inch is just not enough space, consider Bruce Lee's famous "One Inch Punch." With his fist only one inch away from his unfortunate volunteer's chest, he would punch, seeming only to tap the opposite fellow, and send him flying backwards for several yards! So, I think you can produce strong, clean-sounding slurs with a little less wind-up, don't you?

Descending Slurs (Pull-offs)

A descending slur, or pull-off, has the same sort of a "snap" to it, with only a few extra components.

In the two following illustrations, you can see what a secure pull-off looks like, and what an all too common but insecure pull-off looks like.

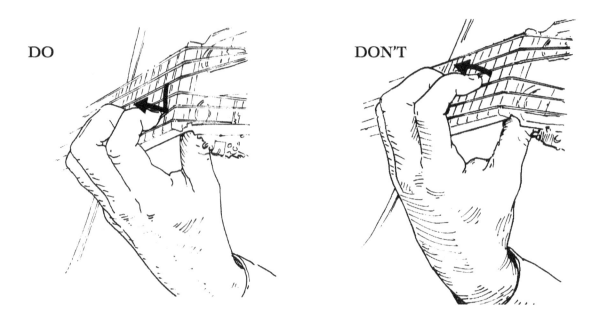

DO   DON'T

In the first example, the finger pulls down into the fingerboard and next string. At first casual glance, it appears as if the finger may indeed be pulling itself off the string; but in reality, we are making the string snap-off of the fingertip. This, of course, causes the finger to pull into the next string, creating a sort of left-hand rest stroke. Use this adjacent string to help our finger empty out, and to spring it back into a ready position above the string.

The second illustration shows a pull-off done habitually by many people. Practically taking the term "pull-off" literally, the finger is pulled upward away from the string and fingerboard, thus creating a consistently feeble tone.

Practice the following slur exercise with these things in mind:

From a state of dynamic relaxation (meaning, in this case, the finger is pressing down just enough to make the note sound), move, or snap, the finger quickly through the string, then spring it back up with a relaxed gesture. Both the snap and the spring are one motion. The finger should not seem to be forced back up. Rather, it is quickly brought back up with the springboard of the string to help you.

Repeat this on each string.

Repeat each example at least 4x.

Finger Independence

It is crucial that the fingers be able to maneuver independently of one another. The following exercises are designed to increase both vertical and horizontal dexterity. Some are also incorporated into the *Daily Warm-up Routine* on page 78.

#1

Put down or "fix" the fingers indicated on the third string. Play the notes indicated with the free finger. It always helps me to think of the fixed fingers as being rooted to the very back of the neck, and the free finger as being as light as a feather. I also prefer practicing these in the fifth position, where the frets are closer together and the horizontal reach is easier and therefore less fatiguing over an extended period of time.

18

#2

Now we will deal with moving two fingers and fixing two fingers. The same principles apply here: rooting the two fixed fingers through to the back of the neck, while keeping the two movable fingers as light as possible. You'll find there's more potential for strain here, so take it slow and focus on the stretch as you extend your fingers, and then on the opposing motion as they pass each other. Finally, sustain the second bass-note as your next finger travels up to the treble, and then hold the second treble-note as you switch to the bass, etc.

#3 - Opposing Motion

You should practice these exercises two ways:

First, play each one *staccato*, with all the notes detached. Let the fingers of your left hand feel the spring upward between fingering changes. Remember not to spring upward any higher than one inch. After your fingers release the notes, instantly place them right above the next two notes. Take your time and play through each variation this way.

The next step is to play them as *legato* as possible, without a noticeable gap between the notes. To do this, stay on the strings until the last possible instant. Visualize your fingers going to the next two notes, then switch.

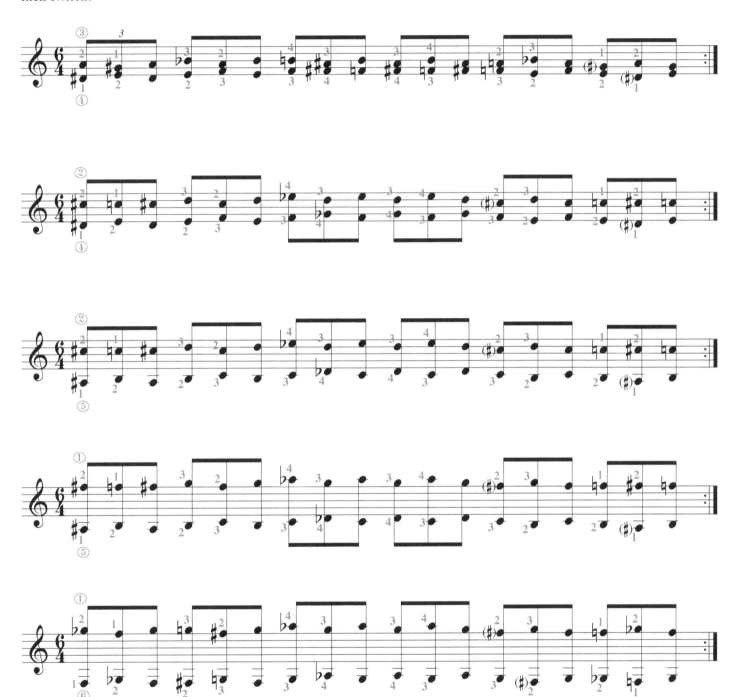

#4 - Horizontal Character Builders

It's exercises such as these that earned this book its title. We're focusing on several things during this next set. First of all, because they're slurs we have to make sure we play them cleanly and with the proper snap. Try to make each one sound clearly. Relaxing or emptying out each finger when it lifts up is very important. Since you're extending your finger across the strings at practically the same moment you're lifting it, there is less time to empty it. This is why I insist that you begin slowly. Start with a metronome setting of ♪ = 60!

We also need to concentrate on extending the fingers. Try to position each finger over its next note right away. Play slowly, but move quickly.

IMPORTANT: If you feel any pain in your hand, wrist, or forearm, stop and rest! Of course, try to distinguish between pain and a little fatigue. The whole point of these exercises is to strengthen your hand, increase stamina and work certain muscles that may not have been worked before. Your hand will be a little tired after each exercise, and this is normal. Pain, however, is not normal, and the only way to get rid of it is to stop playing.

I also suggest you rest for five minutes or more between each exercise until the fatigued feeling goes away. Then you can start again. Either go on to the next one or repeat the one you've just done. If you feel that a particular stretch is impossible for you, skip it. You'll be able to do it in time.

Begin at ♪ = 60

#5 - Odair's Favorite Drill

I'm not really certain that this is his *favorite,* but I did borrow it from Odair Assad and his brother Sergio when they suggested that a student practice this a lot during one of their master classes. It's self-explanatory. Just make sure you hold down the notes where indicated.

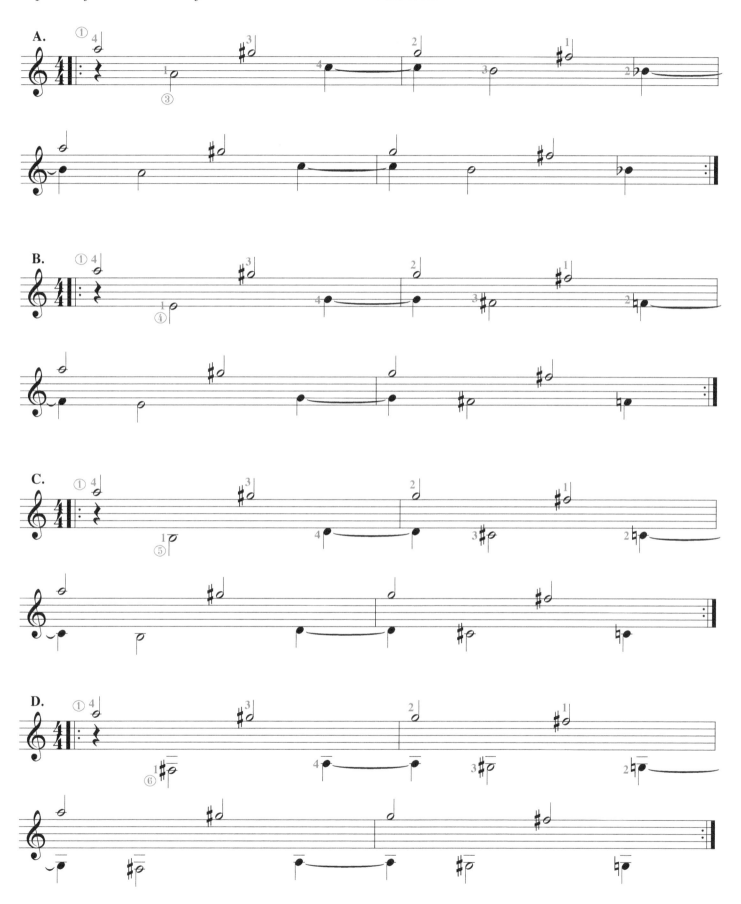

#6 - "The Spider"

Here's a fun one. It's called "the spider" because, when it is played smoothly, your hand resembles a spider crawling up the neck. Isn't that marvelous?! Great at parties. Thrill your kids.

As you lift one pair of fingers, instantly get them into position above the next pair of notes.

continue....

The Barre

Playing lots of barres is always annoying. However, that tired, burning feeling you get between your thumb and first finger is probably just the result of pressing too hard. Also, if you stop to think about it, only rarely does a barre require the entire finger pressed against the fingerboard.

Weight vs. Pressure

First, analyze your barre. Are you allowing the weight of your arm and gravity to assist you? Look at the picture on the right and see how weight should be channeled.

Notice how the angle of the neck, the angle of the forearm, together with the gravity that is pulling on the elbow are combining to naturally channel the weight back into the fingerboard. Believe me, it is much easier to feel it for yourself than trying to put it into words.

Being Selective

The other element you need in solving your barre problem is selectivity. Figure out exactly which notes underneath your finger need to sound. You rarely need every millimeter of your finger squeezing all the time.

Usually you'll find that what makes your finger most uncomfortable is having to straighten it out completely, or applying pressure to the middle joint. Look at this next chord, and play it on your guitar. As you play it, are you clamping your entire finger across all six strings? You shouldn't be. What notes from this chord really need to be played with your first finger?

Answer: the low B on the sixth string, the F♯ on the second, and the B on the first. Just three notes! So in this case you don't have to lock your middle joint. In fact, you can relax it, thus creating a barre that makes your finger look curved.

Now here's a good one for you!

Lightly barre the seventh fret. Play each note written by applying pressure only to the appropriate part of your finger. Sometimes you'll find the string coinciding with a crease in your finger. If this happens, gently roll or move your finger slightly until the note sounds clearly. Since everyone's fingers are different, we all have to experiment for ourselves.

Summing It All Up

It seems to me that the main cause of many peoples' hand problems and pain is the retention of tension. They hold the tension in their fingers and hand while they shift, change notes, or any other time they are not actually playing a note. There is no reason for this aside from technical insecurity. Know what you're hand is doing at all times, which fingers are pressing and which are not—be totally aware. This is the first and most important step towards a secure technique. What you do or don't do in between the notes means everything.

Quadrivial Quandary by Andrew York— A Four-Voice Study for the Left Hand

Here's an exquisite little chord study that Andy has written for the left hand. There are just a few things to keep in mind while working on it:

1. Take your time—a slow tempo and quick, accurate movements are the key.
2. Always visualize the next chord in your mind's eye before moving there.
3. Observe all held notes.
4. Although the ideal tempo is ♩ = 80, begin much slower and without a metronome. A metronome would force you to stay with the beat and move to the next chord whether you are ready or not.

Quadrivual Quandary
Track 2

Andrew York

Andante (Legato)
♩ = 80 - 92

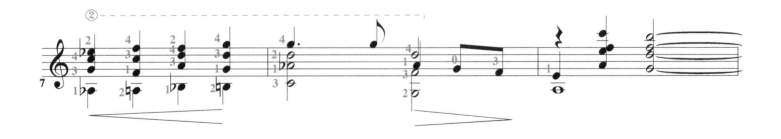

27

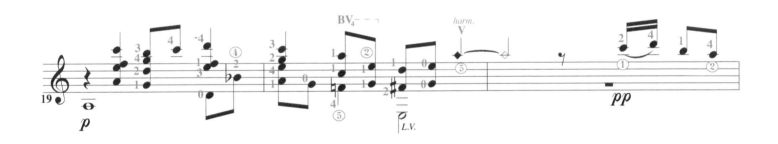

"Fanfare"
A Slur Study by Brian Head

Brian's *Fanfare* is not only a great slur work-out, it's appropriate for a concert program, too. Technically, it contains a good balance of slurs and opposing motions. Focus on the following:

1. Practice slowly and execute all slurs accurately with a good, solid tone.
2. Make sure that all held notes are sustained during any other slur activity.
3. Take note of the meter changes.

Fanfare

Brian Head

"May the Notes Be with You," A Slur Study by Evan Hirschelman

This is a two-movement work with an emphasis on varying slur techniques. The first movement is a combination of descending slurs and arpeggios, creating a flowing *campanella* (Italian for "little bells," because the notes ring through each other) effect. Some of the phrases are indeterminate in regards to the number of repetitions, allowing the performer to adjust the phrase's length according to their own personal interpretation. The second movement is very rhythmic. It utilizes most types of slurs, such as ascending and descending, combinations with fixed fingers, double stops, left-hand only, muted slurs, and more.

– Evan Hirschelman

1st Movement — What You Should Do

- Hold notes as long as possible, which might make certain shifts more challenging but will result in a more flowing texture.

- The shift into measure 44 should be played in time, which requires a quicker shifting motion than elsewhere in the movement.

- The tenuto markings can sometimes be interpreted as a very subtle fermata but they will also emphasize the melodic transitions.

2nd Movement — What You Should Do

- In measure 1, dampen the low open D with back of right-hand thumb while plucking the 4th-string D (third note in pattern).

- Hammering on the 5th-string D (5th note in measure 1) naturally dampens the open A before it. This takes place each time this pattern occurs with an eighth note rest below the group.

May the Notes Be with You

Track 4

I.

Evan Hirschelman

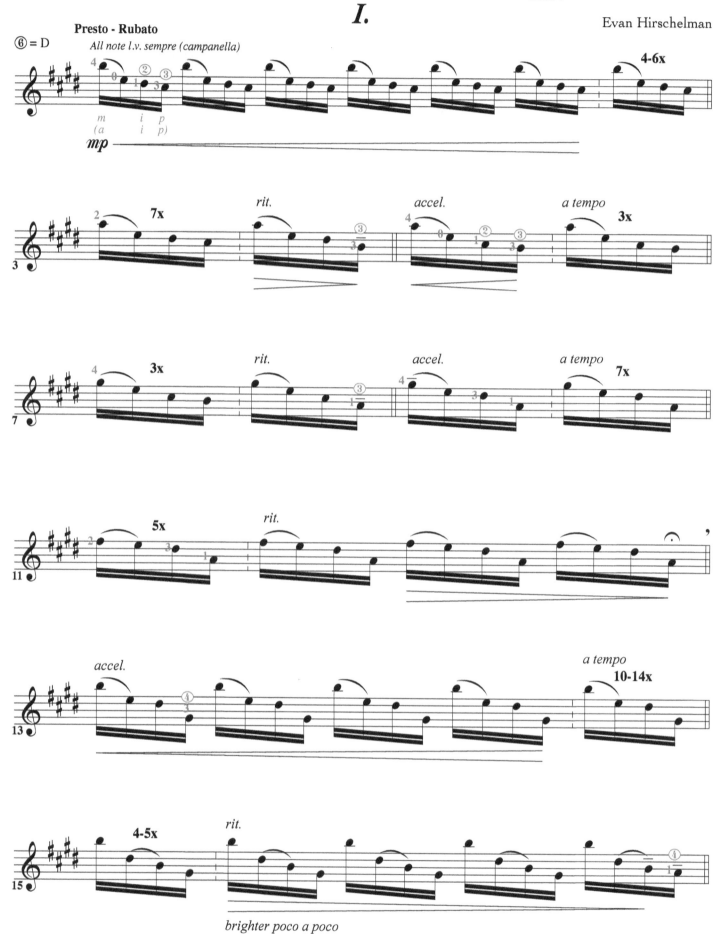

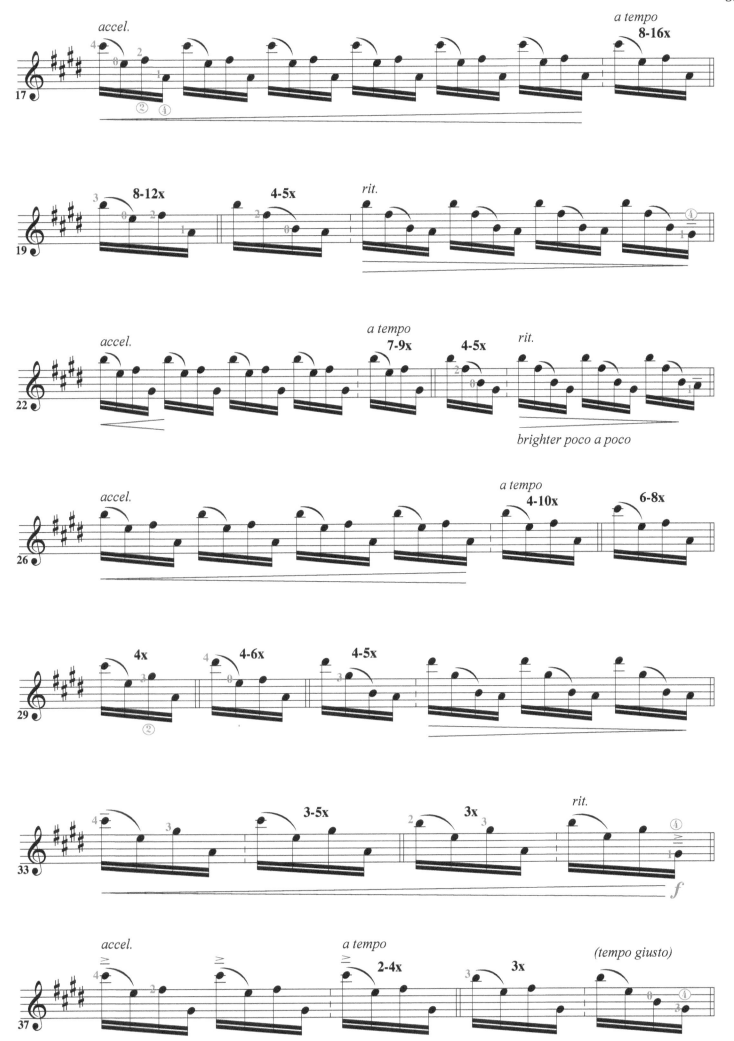

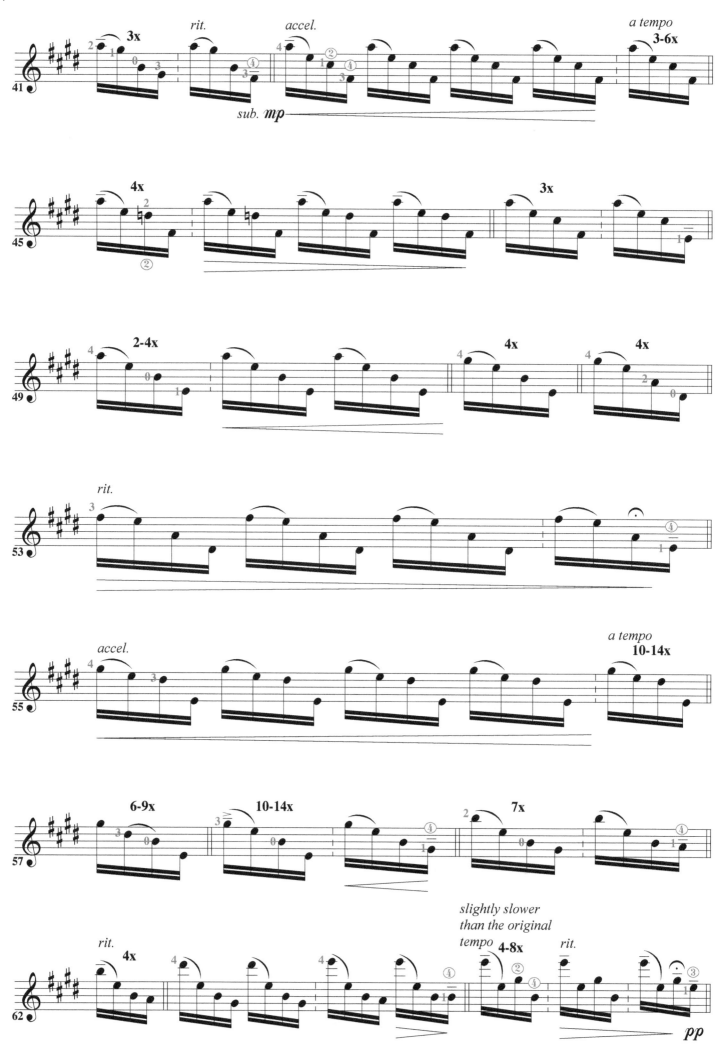

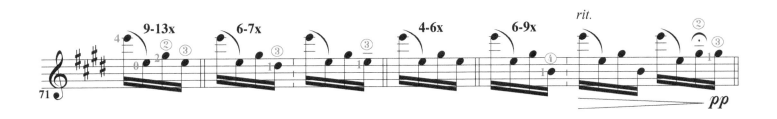

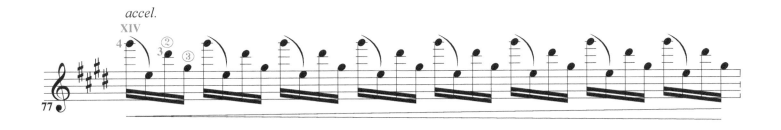

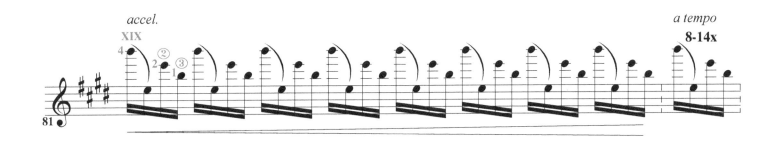

INTRODUCTION

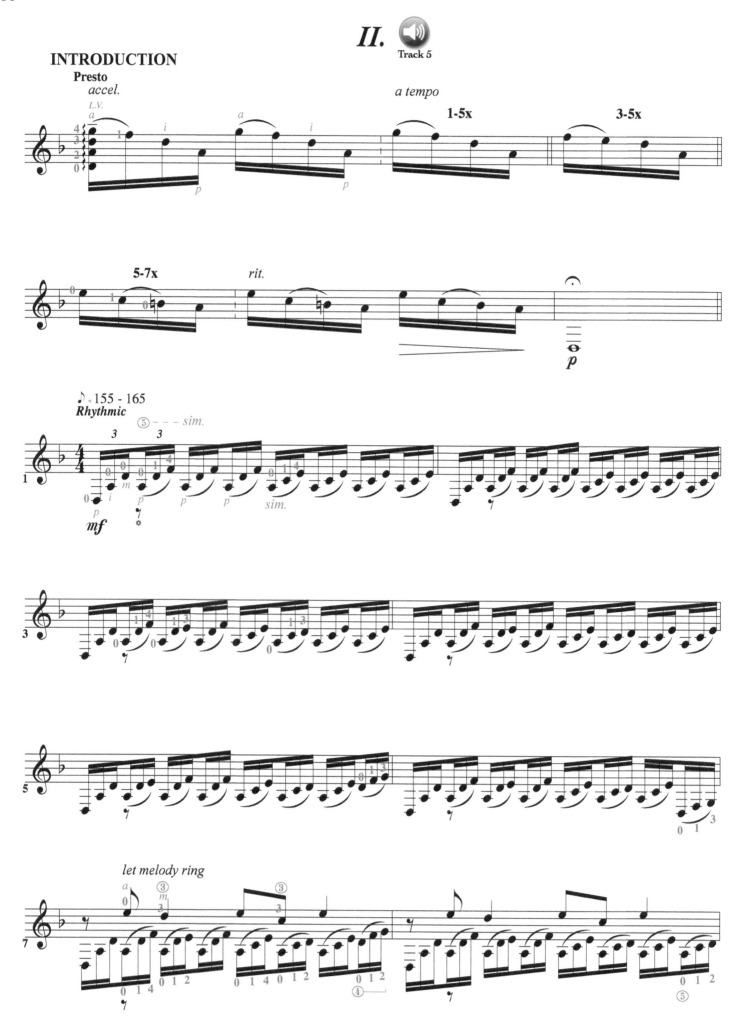

II. Track 5

* With this rest, the composer is emphasizing that the previous bass note should be stopped.

* 1/2 slur is a hammer-on from nowhere

"DO or DO NOT; there is no TRY"

• Yoda •

Giuliani's Left-Hand Etudes, Op. 1

I remember practicing these diligently from the age of 12 all the way through my college years and beyond. I still single out one or two of these time and again for improving my left-hand agility and accuracy. I consider them to be exceptionally helpful for technique, as long as they are practiced with focus and attention is paid to finger placement and movement.

These are from Mauro Giuliani's Opus 1 collection, which also included the *120 Right-Hand Studies* found starting on page 111 of this book.

The left-hand fingerings are those of the composer's. Although you may find there are more convenient ways to finger them, I would stick with Maestro Mauro's suggestions. They are not necessarily fingered for musical fluidity; their purpose is to move the fingers and give them a workout.

What You Should Do

To take full advantage of the effectiveness of these exercises, focus on the following points:

- Hold the fingered notes for their full value, moving off them at the last possible moment for maximum reduction/elimination of spaces between the changes. Keep it smooth.

- Feel that you are "aiming and throwing" the fingers, rather than "lifting and pressing" them down. Aiming and throwing will enable the fingers to relax more when they get to their notes, while lifting and pressing will lead to prolonged finger tension.

- Whenever possible, lightly hover the fingers which are to play next over their notes; or at least envision them magnetically being drawn there. For instance, in Etude No. 1, measure 3, while plucking the open G and B strings, get fingers 4 and 2 in position over the next notes—F♯ and A. This isn't always possible, but it will help with both your visualization skills and readiness of the fingers. Both are good habits.

- As per the composer's instructions, try playing the patterns with *p* and *i* of the right hand, although I have found that *p* and *m* ultimately work better for me. Either way, we're focusing on the left hand here, and it's best to keep the right-hand fingering very simple.

- Start slowly, thinking of the notes as eighth notes, or even fast quarter notes, rather than 16ths. How you move and play the notes is by far more important than playing fast. These aren't speed tests. You will be able play them fast soon enough if you control what your fingers do in the spaces between the notes.

No. 1

No. 2

No. 3

No. 4

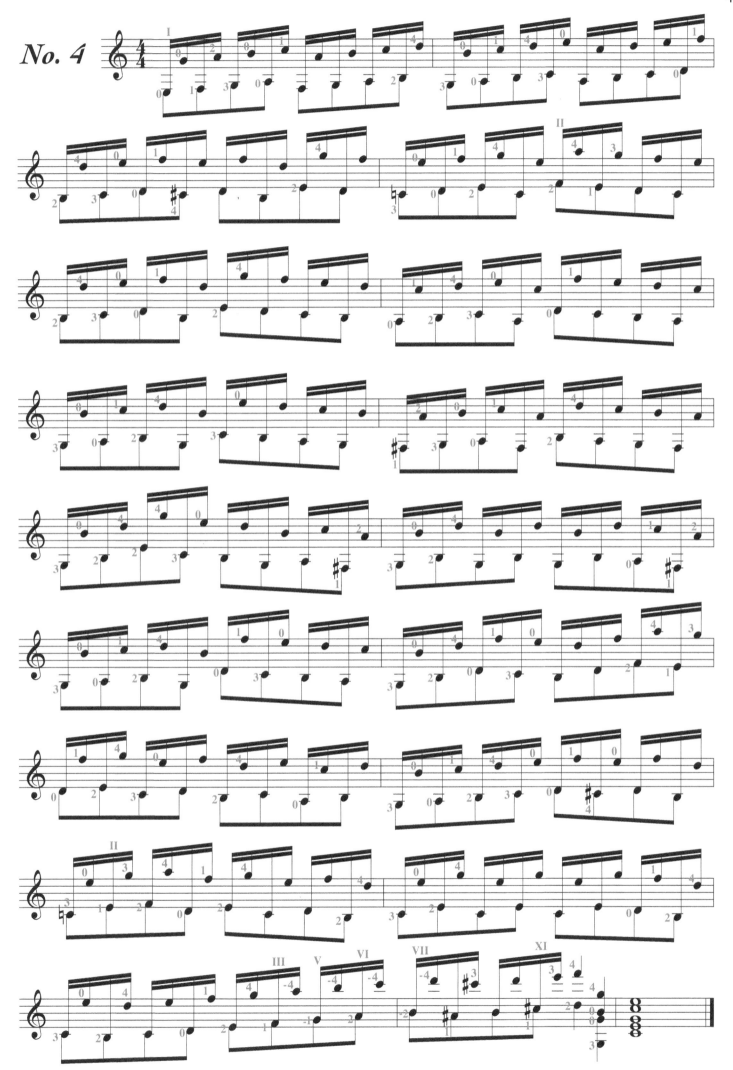

46

No. 5

No. 6

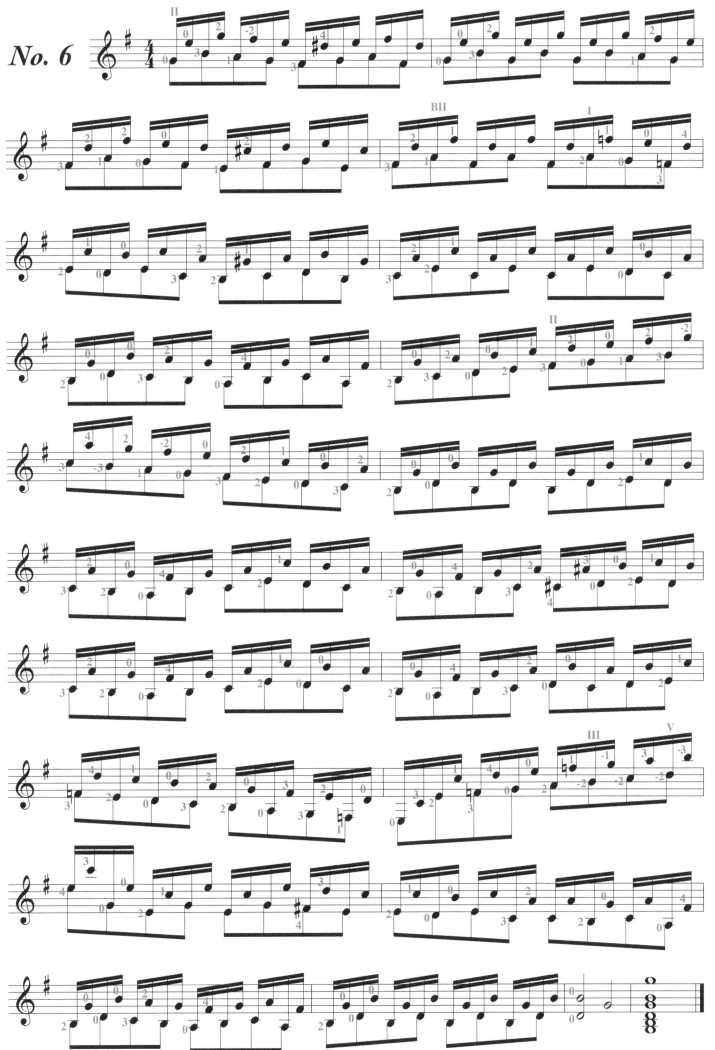

No. 7

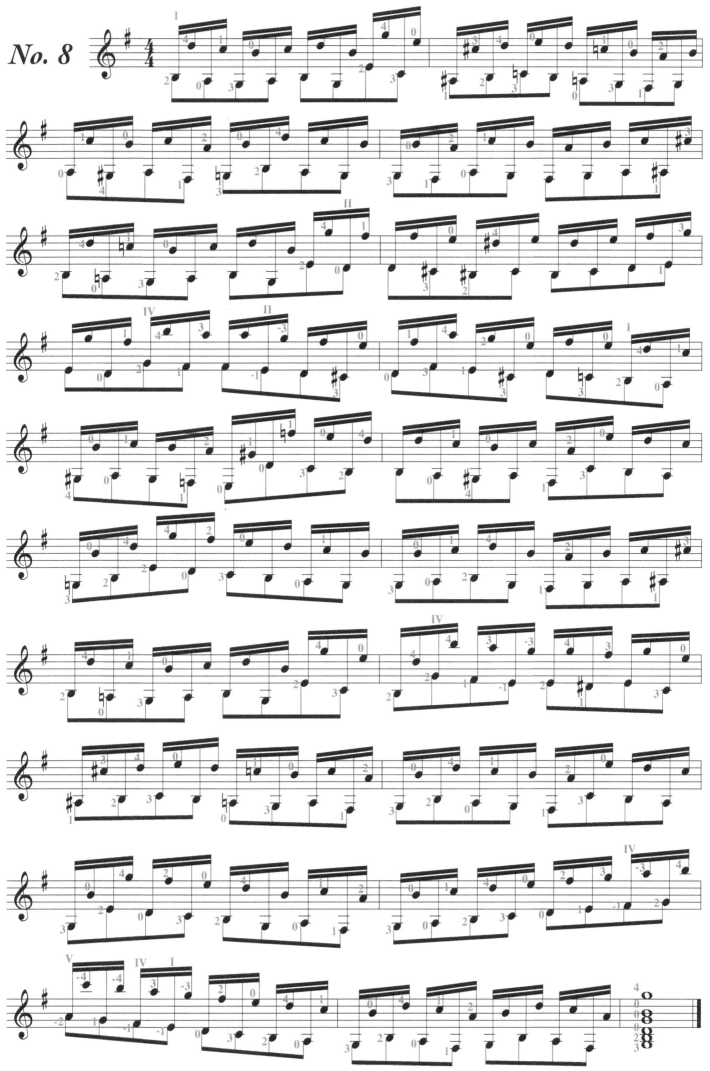

No. 8

No. 9

No. 11

No. 12

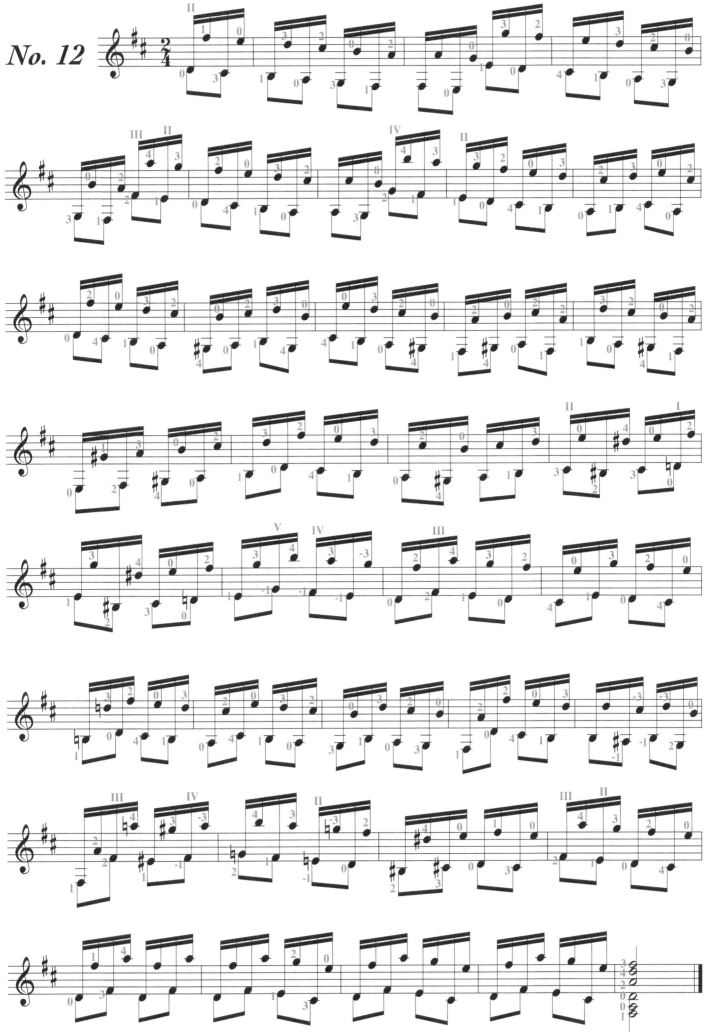

No. 13

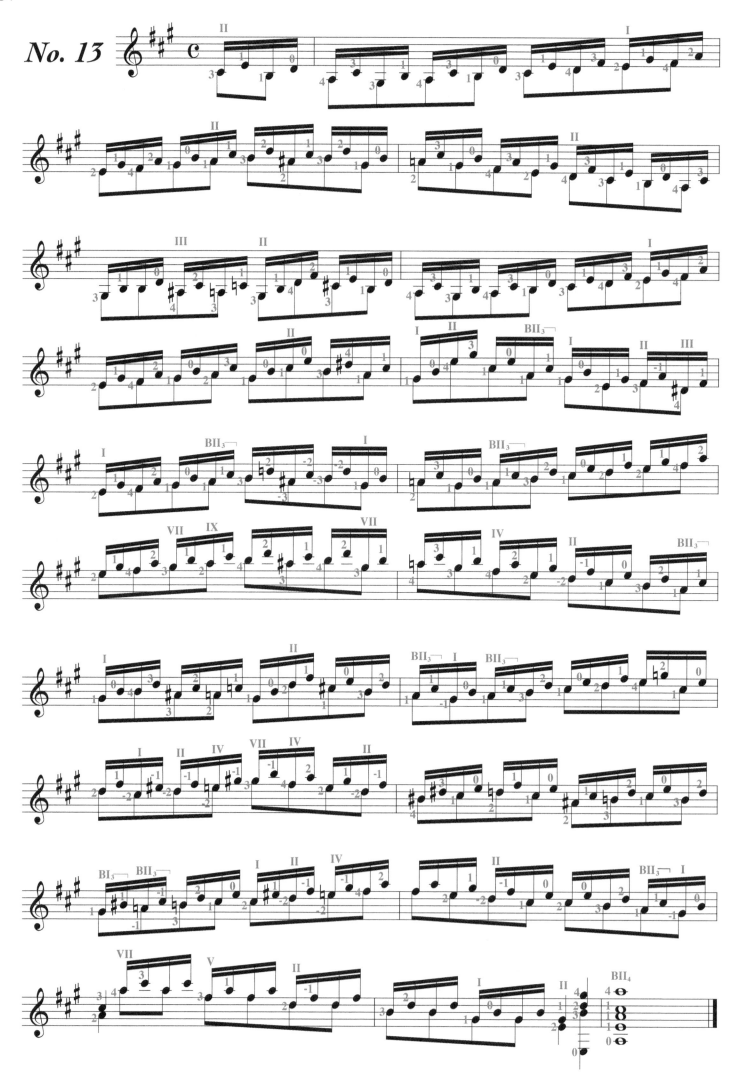

No. 14

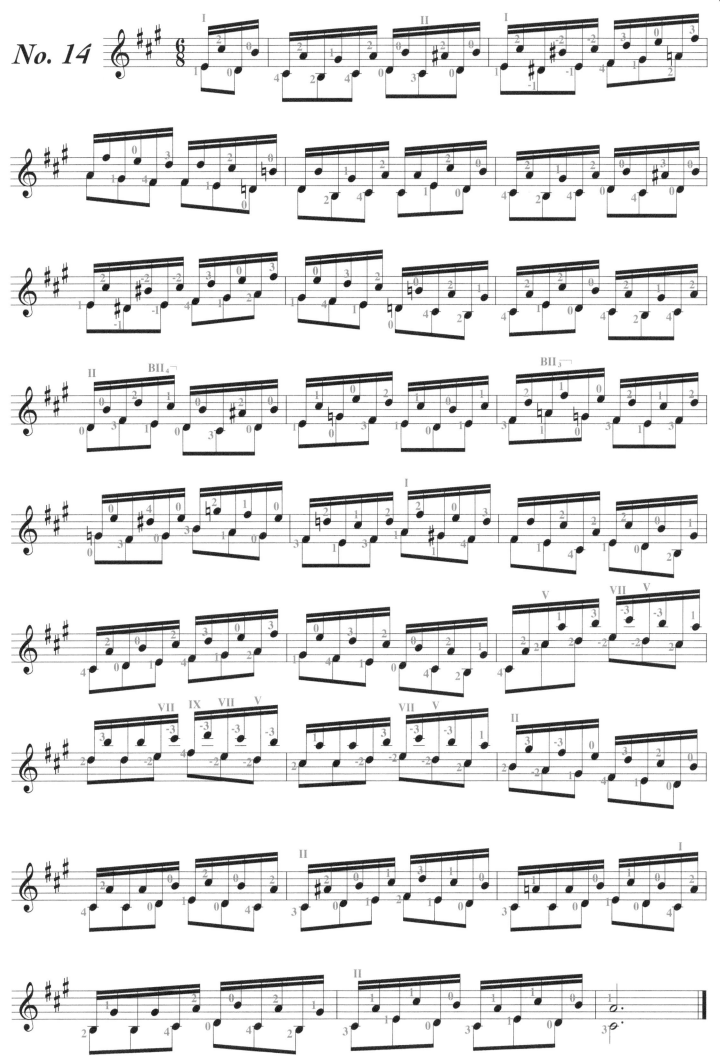

No. 15

No. 16

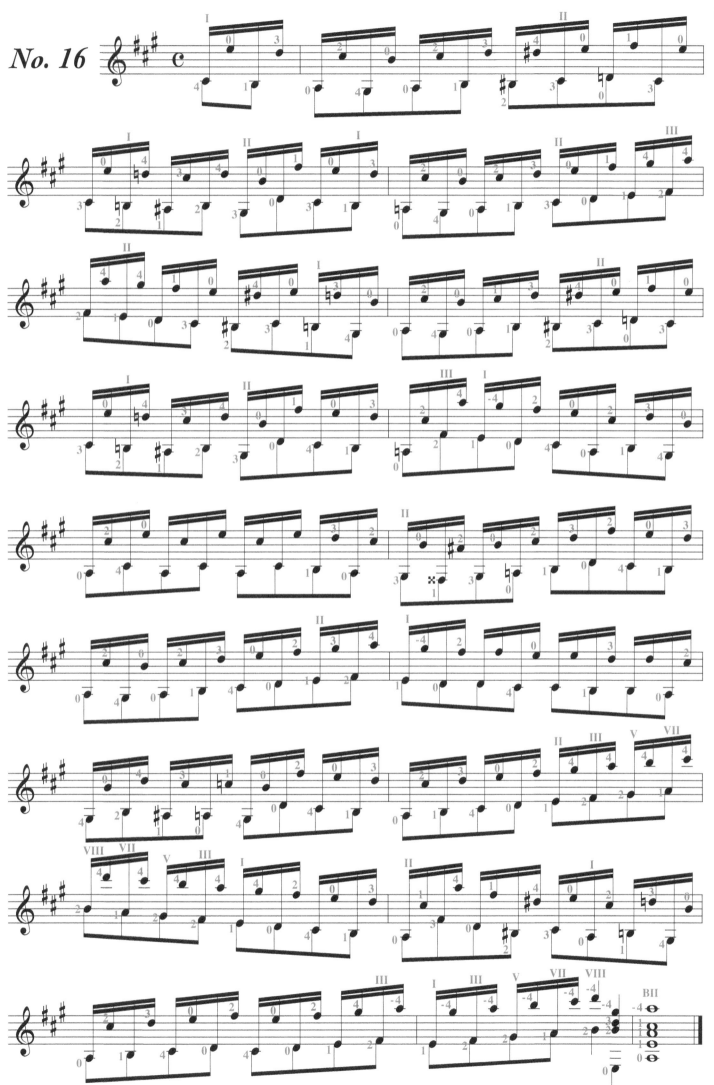

THE RIGHT HAND

Tone Production

The right hand produces sound. Although the quality of tone is determined by both hands, the type of tone and the volume are controlled primarily by the right hand.

There are seven ingredients that go into tone production:

1. Nail length and shape.
2. Choice of stroke: free stroke or rest stroke.
3. Hand position and the angle of the fingers to the strings.
4. How the fingertip and nail approach the string.
5. How the fingertip and nail prepare on the string.
6. Finger pressure against the string.
7. The release of the fingertip and nail from the string.

Each of these ingredients influences all the others. One will generally determine what comes next. For instance, your choice of rest stroke or free stroke will determine your hand position, and therefore the angle of the finger to the string. This will then determine how the finger approaches the string, and thus how the finger is finally prepared on the string. All of these contribute to the security of the fingers on the string and your ability to apply the appropriate pressure; and the pressure inevitably effects how the string will be released. The length and shape of the fingernail effects how successfully you will be able to carry out all of the various parts of the stroke.

Nail Length and Shape

If a nail is too long, the speed and ease with which the fingertip and nail go through the string is considerably diminished. This is because the resistance has been increased. A bad nail shape can also create undesirable resistance against the string and cause some very interesting but unsavory sounds.

The reason we play with our fingernails at all is to assist us in securing and controlling the string, to enhance our volume and tone.   So it is important that you grow and shape them in a way that will make it easier to play and sound good.

The following illustrations show some different nail types and ways to shape them. You'll also see how to gauge their length.

Nail Length

To gauge the length of your nail, hold your finger out horizontally and then place a file against the fingertip at a right angle. If the nail and flesh touch the file at about the same time, the length is good. If you have to tilt the file forward or back the nail is either too long or too short.

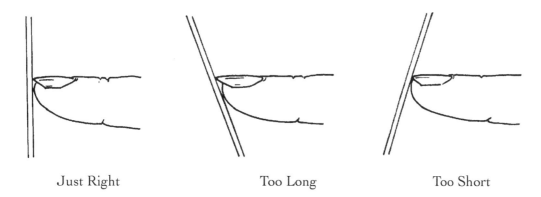

Just Right   Too Long   Too Short

Nail Types

These nail types represent the four basic shapes: curved (Type A), flat (Type B), hooked downward (Type C) and bent upwards (Type D). While the curved shape is ideal, the latter three shapes are the most common.

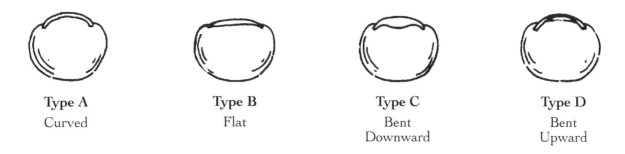

Type A
Curved

Type B
Flat

Type C
Bent
Downward

Type D
Bent
Upward

Here are the basic "do's and don'ts" for shaping the nails:

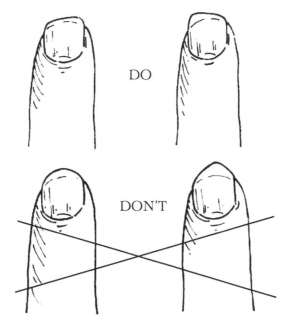

DO

DON'T

There are various reasons why a nail shape will be either advantageous or not. One of the most important issues is how the string moves across the nail. Shapes #1 and #2 to the right (the "don'ts" from the bottom of page 59) cause the string to travel "uphill" with too much resistance. These shapes also prevent us from using enough of the nail, since they release near the middle of the nail.

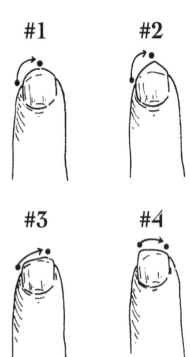

Either of the two shapes (#3 and #4) shown on the right allow the string to travel along a "ramp" and release from the nail more easily, at the same time using the maximum amount of nail possible. Your nail type will determine which of these two shapes is best for you, but they both enable the string to travel along desirable ramps.

The old advice that we should file our nails to match the contour of their fingertips just doesn't always work. Although it may not look all that bad to you, what the string "sees" from its angle is a hill that has to be climbed. Sometimes if it is rounded too much, as in shape #2, a point develops, creating even greater resistance and a more abrupt release point. This is absolutely devastating if your nail is a Type C, or "hooked" nail. With shapes #1 or #2, the hook is exaggerated instead of minimized.

Nail shapes #3 and #4 are both good, but have different effects. Shape #3 is most common and advantageous, as it aids in pushing the string into the soundboard during a stroke. This generally results in a fuller sound. Because the ramp is angled upwards, this shape can result in much more resistance (nail to string) than shape #4. As you can see, shape #4 is angled slightly downwards, making the string travel downhill during a stroke. This allows for a very fast, smooth release; so fast, in fact, it makes some players feel that their finger is slipping off the string. Many players who use rest stroke primarily, and who play at less of an angle to the string, prefer this shape, while those who prefer using free stroke favor the #3.

If you have had a problem finding a good shape to match your nail type, the following page contains some matches you may find useful.

Nail Type	Shape

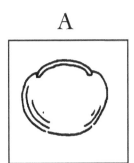

A

#3   #4

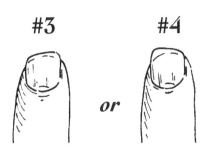

or

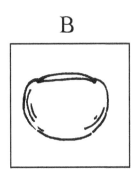

B

#3   #4

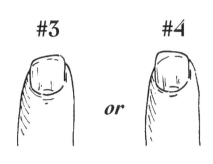

or

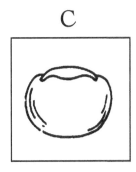

C

#3

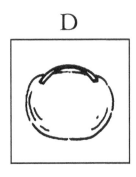

D

#3   #4

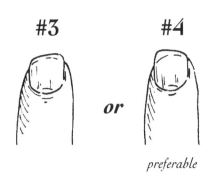

or

preferable

Shaping the Nails

Always use a file, as opposed to a nail cutter, to shape the fingernails of your right hand. Nail cutters leave the fibers of your nails with jagged ends, even if you polish with sandpaper afterwards.

Always file your nails with your fingertips facing you. Position the file underneath the nail at a slight angle and look down the surface of the file. This gives you the ideal view of the edge of the nail. Try to create a straight line as seen from this angle, as illustrated on the right.

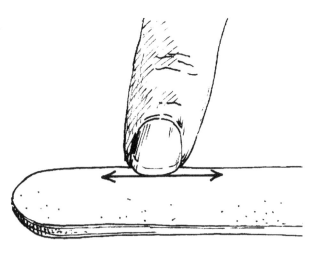

Ideally, the file will touch the edge of the nail evenly across its width, and fit securely underneath it without rocking around. If the shape of your nail is too round, you will notice a rocking motion as the file moves around the nail's edge.

The line illustrated to the right will only be seen from this particular angle. The nail shape is not actually straight or flat. It will still appear rounded, although possibly not as round as the fleshy fingertip.

These ideas for shaping your nails are only suggestions. There are many variations on the four nail types discussed in this book. While I have found that the corresponding shapes suggested here work well consistently, experimentation is encouraged. Find out what works and feels best for you.

Angle and Placement

In order to achieve a full, or "fat" tone, we must give special attention to the angle of the fingertips to the strings. Note that when the fingers are initially placed on the strings, only the flesh makes contact. The nail makes its contact when pressure is applied. The illustration below shows an advantageous angle.

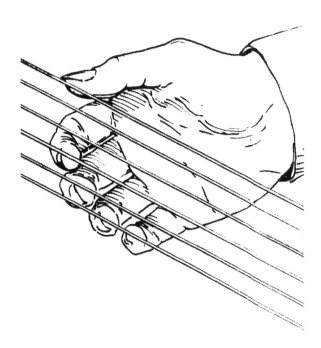

When a finger moves straight back into the palm from this angle, it is actually moving over a healthy portion of the string surface (as the string uses the nail as a "ramp") which enhances the tone. This angle, however, creates a scraping sound on the wound bass strings, and should therefore be adjusted to a straighter angle for playing on the fourth, fifth and sixth strings.

Rest Stroke (Apoyando)

What a rest stroke really does is set the string vibrating more in the direction of the soundboard. Physically, this results in more resonance inside the guitar and on the soundboard itself. This is why a rest stroke is generally perceived to be fuller sounding than a free stroke.

Position

The large joint, which is where the main thrust of the stroke originates, is placed over the next lower adjacent string. For instance, if you are playing the first string, the large joint should hover above the second or third.

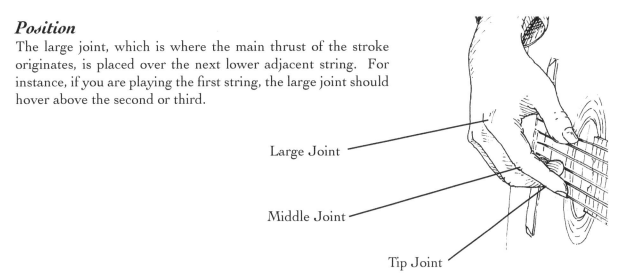

Large Joint

Middle Joint

Tip Joint

The Movement

Although all of the joints in the finger move, the joint that actually moves the finger is the large joint (the metacarpophalangeal). This is the source of the thrust that pushes the finger through the string. It's also the only joint that moves the finger in towards the hand, allowing for a big round sound. The others move the fingertip upwards, which, if we restricted the movement at the large joint, would cause a thin sound. Think of it as similar to legs walking: we propel ourselves forward from our hip, not our knees or ankles.

Although they all take place in such rapid succession that they blend themselves together into one movement, there are three steps involved in every stroke:

1. Planting (preparation)
2. Pressure
3. Release

Planting

Planting simply involves preparing, or placing, a fingertip on a string accurately enough to execute a stroke (see the illustration above). It also helps to briefly stop the vibration of a string between notes—just enough to control the tone. Slapping the finger down onto a vibrating string causes a slapping sound, and, more often than not, the nail alone makes careless string contact creating a sizzling effect. By planting we control where we land and minimize any unpleasant noises.

Planting the fingers is also the only effective way to control articulation. Those who claim they never plant their fingers, and in fact actually teach their students not to plant, maintain that planting a finger stops the sound, which is undesirable. This, of course, is true when the preparation is exaggerated, as we do when we are first learning how it is done. But planting gets much more advanced than that. Anyone who makes a good sound, who can control their tone and articulation, and has any kind of developed awareness of what their fingers are doing, is planting their fingers to some extent.

Pressure

The pressure we put on a string displaces it to some degree. The distance we move a string in one direction determines how far it will go in the other direction. This establishes how loud a note will be. No matter what amount of pressure you put on a string, always make sure you feel the string move underneath your finger. Be aware!

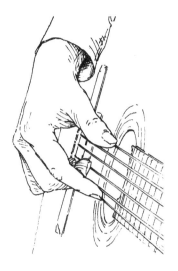
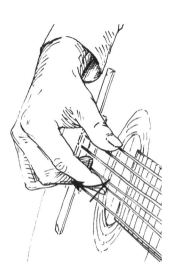

Release

The release is what determines the sound. In the case of a rest stroke, the finger simply uses the pressure it has applied to pull through the string, emptying out as it comes in contact with the adjacent string. Emptying the finger aids in springing it back into place for the next note. Notice how a well-executed rest stroke goes in towards the soundboard.

Free Stroke (Tirando)

A free stroke is essentially the same as a rest stroke in that the setup and movement are similar. One could justifiably describe a rest stroke as an interrupted free stroke, or a free stroke as a rest stroke with follow-through.

There are two important things to strive for during a free stroke:
1. Set the string vibrating into the soundboard as much as possible.
2. The finger should follow-through straight back toward the heel of the hand.

These elements help optimize the potential for a full sound. A well-executed free stroke can be just as strong as a rest stroke.

The drawings below show a good free stroke. Notice that the large joint is positioned above the string it is playing (as opposed to being over the next lower string, as in rest stroke). This allows for optimum string displacement and a good follow-through. If this joint is back any further than this, the probability of the smaller joints pulling upwards more to bypass the next string increases. Avoid this and keep the main thrust coming from the large joint.

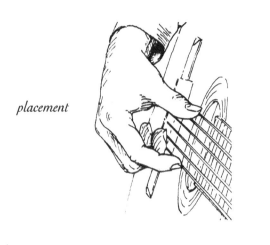

placement

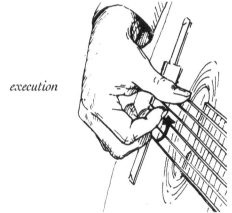

execution

Right-Hand Finger Independence

Walking

Great as a daily warmup, or when used as technical practice, the following "walking" exercise is simple yet effective. It is probably one of the most effective exercises in this book. After realizing that the main obstacle keeping me from progressing in my scales was crossing strings, I started "walking." I practiced only crossing strings—and it worked! I still practice this every day, and my scales now feel secure. In fact, when I do hit a snag, I'll work on the right-hand string crossing all by itself (see Problem Solving in Scales on page 103).

Here are the things you should keep in mind:

1. Do the exercise using rest stroke and free stroke. Rest stroke is the more challenging of the two.
2. As soon as you release one note, place your finger on the next string *immediately*.
3. Always strive to produce a good, solid tone.

If you focus on these three things, you'll get results. Make sure you practice with one finger at first, then alternating two (or even three) fingers. I would suggest spending the first few practice sessions working on the one-finger drills. Focusing intensely for 5 to 15 minutes should be good enough. Spend longer if you wish, but concentrate. Then, move on to the *i–m* alternation. I mainly stick with *i* and *m* because that's how I finger most of my scales; but by all means, make up your own patterns, especially if you like playing your scales with three fingers instead of two.

Variations

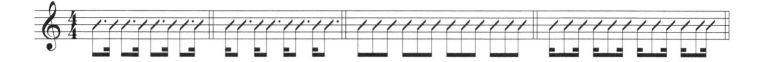

Also, try playing the first note rest-stroke, the next one free-stroke, the next rest-stroke, and so on. In addition, practicing your scales with just one finger is great!

Arpeggios from Tarrega's
The Complete Technical Studies

These are great exercises for developing your finger independence. They involve standard finger combinations in the context of awkward string crossings.

Practice using free stroke, with a full sound. Wherever string crossing is involved, make sure you prepare the next note immediately after releasing the last.

If you are one of the multitude of players who have difficulty playing a thumb rest stroke while doing free strokes with your fingers, this is a good opportunity to work on that technique.

Take your time. It is best to work on a few of these during a practice session, and become comfortable with them before moving on. You don't necessarily have to play them all every day.

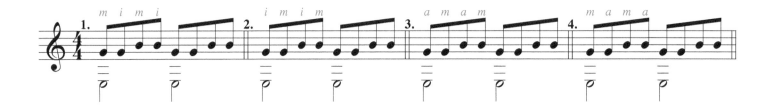

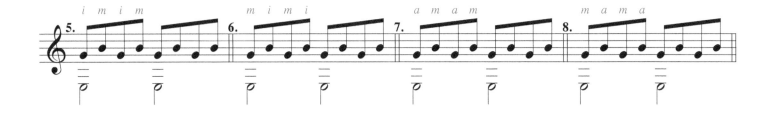

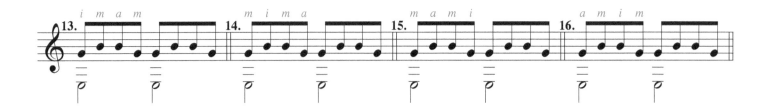

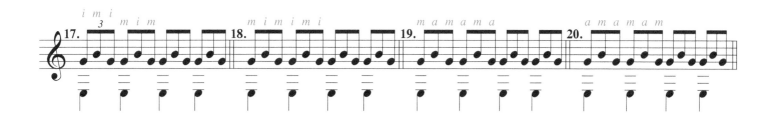

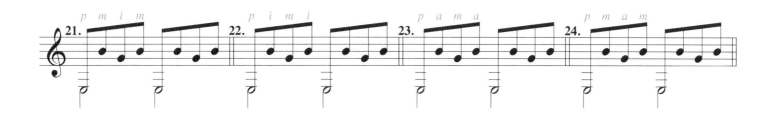

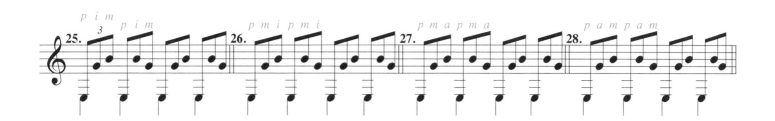

The Thumb

Just as the fingers move from the large joint, the thumb moves primarily from the wrist joint. The tip joint moves to aid in the follow-through, or to help produce a desired tone or effect.

The thumb also moves the string in toward the soundboard before releasing.

NOTE: For a free stroke, the string is displaced downward, and the thumb releases low, close to the soundboard.

COMMON MISTAKE: The thumb displaces the string parallel to the top, and releases high.

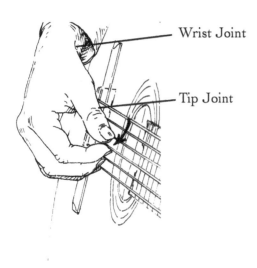

Wrist Joint

Tip Joint

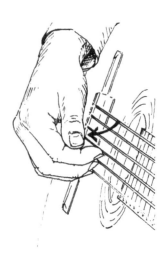

Shaping the Nail

The shape of your thumbnail should allow the thumb to play the string easily, without catching.

The illustration below shows a good shape. It won't catch on the string; in fact, it almost fits evenly against the string. However, a more rounded fingertip will require less of a slant, while a more tapered fingertip may require more. This thumbnail shape also allows for greater control of tone colors, since it makes it easy to switch from an "all-nail" tone to an "all-flesh" tone, or play with the standard "flesh/nail" combination.

Develop That Thumb!

Many players tend to sentence the thumb to confinement in the bass. The logical association of the thumb with the bass aside, there really is no reason to forgo the development of this prized appendage! Most of our thumbs are weak and lacking in agility. It's time to let them out for some air and exercise! Also, we should explore some less ordinary uses for the thumb.

The thumb is the most awkward of our manual protrudences—that's true. But strengthening this finger can only help the other parts of your hand. A balanced hand is a happy hand.

Most of us have trouble executing consistently good thumb rest strokes. At first, try playing this next exercise entirely with *p* rest stroke. Then try playing just the first note of each triplet with rest stroke, and the third (after the slur) with free stroke. Controlling the alternation of rest and free strokes is not only a basic technical skill, but it is something you will use over and over again in your musical interpretations.

Take a look at the next chapter, "Flamenco Techniques," to learn more about what the thumb can do.

Balance in Chords

"Balancing Act" is a study designed to help you develop control of the right-hand fingers through regulation of finger pressure on the strings. The *ossia staff* (smaller, alternate staff) shows the note that should be stressed in each chord.

Here are the things you should keep in mind:

1. Make sure the first three and final two chords of the study are well-balanced, with all notes even in volume and tone. Feel each string depressed equally.

2. Bring out the indicated note in each chord by applying more pressure to that string.

3. Start by applying equal pressure to all the strings involved—feel them displaced equally. Then, with the right-hand finger corresponding to the note to be accentuated, displace (move) that string down a little more than the others. Release and follow through. The finger that presses down more should follow-through a little more than the others. Try to feel it rather than think about it.

NOTE:

The tactile awareness required to focus this way is not only important for bringing out certain notes, but for successful and secure playing in general. It's often the missing link between a "good" player and a "great" player.

Balancing Act

Track 6

Scott Tennant

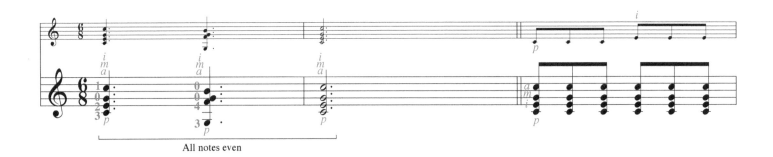

All notes even

All notes even

FLAMENCO TECHNIQUES

What Else Can the Thumb Do?

Flamenco! Included in the bottomless bag of tricks of flamenco guitarists is the way they use their thumbs. Far from trickery, though, the thumb is used mostly out of necessity. The guitarist must be heard through all the singing, hand-clapping, and the piercing footwork that is flamenco. Many fast passages that we classical guitarists would play with our fingers are easily done with the thumb by the flamenco guitarist.

Although not always directly applicable to the classical repertoire, practicing some of the techniques will expand our capabilities. As an example, here is a falsetta from a *Soleares* that was taught to me years ago by the incredible Juan Serrano. This is the exact right hand fingering he used—practically all thumb. All thumb strokes are played rest stroke. And YES!, it is possible!

Soleares Falseta

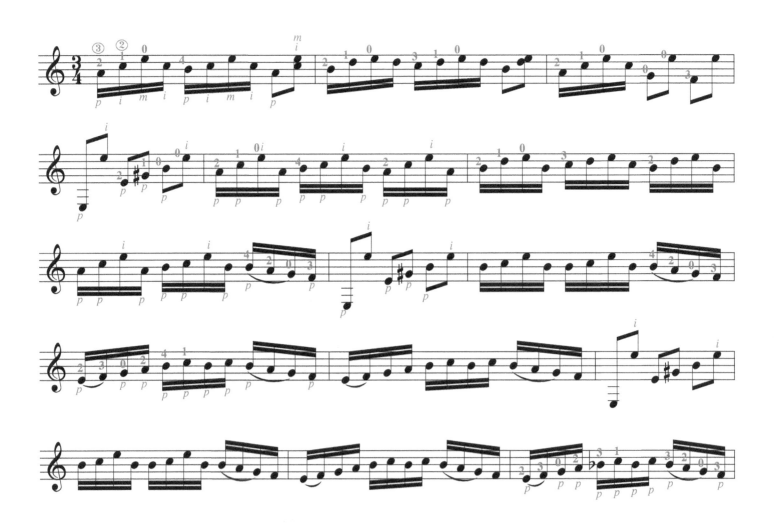

(continued)

Alzapua

Alzapua is a technique which utilizes the back of the nail, as well. It comes from the Spanish word *alzar*, meaning *to lift*. It is a powerful technique, and does wonders for strengthening the thumb.

The arrows pointing up indicate that the thumb goes down (towards the floor) through the strings. The arrows pointing down indicate that the thumb moves upwards (towards the ceiling) through the strings. The key is to move the thumb quickly, trying to sound all the notes simultaneously. If you can hear separations between the notes, you're moving through the strings too slowly. All single notes must be played with thumb rest strokes.

Alzapua Falseta

Rasgueados

This is another flamenco technique which is sadly neglected by many classical guitarists. A *rasguaedo* is really more of a percussive effect than a strum. It is done by hitting the strings with the backs of the nails.

Practicing rasgueados develops the extensor muscles, which are the muscles that move the fingers outward, away from the palm. Many players believe that playing scales with considerable speed and accuracy is dependent upon how quickly we can move our fingers out, not in. This would certainly explain why most flamenco guitarists have the ability to play blazingly fast scales.

For now, practice your rasgueados by anchoring your thumb on the fourth string as you play on the first, second and third strings. It is helpful to begin by alternating only two fingers. Play the examples on the next page with the indicated alternation combinations.

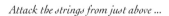

Attack the strings from just above ...   *... not like this.*

On page 75 there are some rasgueado patterns that include all of the fingers. Some are traditional patterns, and some are a little out of the ordinary.

The letter *"c"* indicates the little finger (the pinky, *chiquito* in Spanish). For all the examples except numbers 3 and 6, keep the fingers extended until they have all finished playing.

Examples 8 through 12 involve an exchange between the thumb and the fingers (either all together or individually). This requires a particular motion of the wrist. The wrist should remain as straight as possible while pivoting, as if turning a doorknob. As the thumb plays its upstroke, the fingers follow it into a ready position. As the fingers play the downstroke(s), the thumb follows them into a ready position. In Examples 10 through 12, the thumb returns to a ready position only after *i* has played.

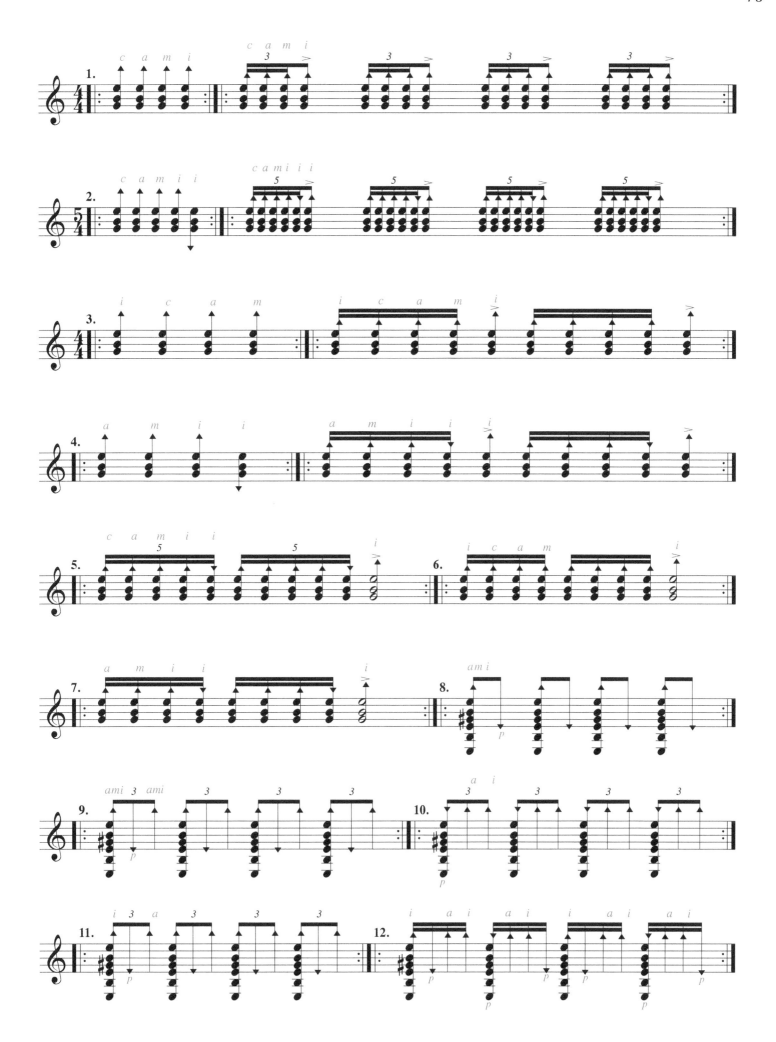

Some Practical Applications

The weight and textures that good rasgueados add to one's playing are substantial. The Spanish repertoire particularly benefits from it. I have included just a few excerpts from Turina and Rodrigo where some alternate right hand patterns are particularly beneficial. But please be aware that these are solutions that work well for myself, and as your skills become sharper, so will your own problem-solving capabilities.

from Turina's "Sevillana"

from Turina's "Ráfaga"

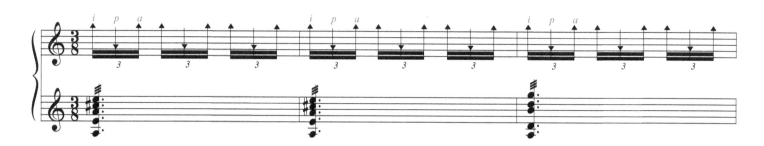

Or, if you want to emphasize the chord changes:

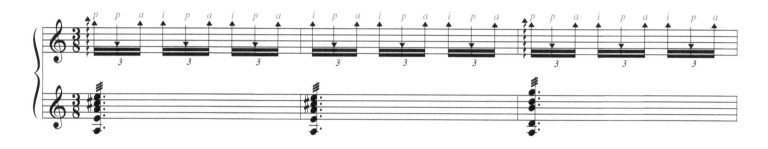

from "Rodrigo's Concerto de Aranjuez, 2nd Movement"

Or:

DAILY WARM-UP ROUTINE

The following exercises have been compiled to form an effective daily technical routine. I would suggest going through the whole thing initially, and noticing where your particular weaknesses lie. You can then isolate those exercises that will strengthen them. On the other hand, I find going through the entire set to be a great warmup.

Left-Hand Walking — #1, #2 & #3

GOALS:
1. Remember the basic left-hand position.
2. Keep right-hand fingering simple and keep the focus on the left hand.
3. Avoid playing with the pads of the fingers or right on the fingertips (refer to the hand position illustration on page 12).
4. Strive for consistent accuracy rather than speed.
5. Move quickly between notes, avoiding gaps in the sound.

#1

#2

#3

Here are some rhythmic variations to apply to #1 and #2.

Ascending Slurs — #4

GOALS:

1. Move the fingers quickly rather than from a great distance.
2. *Empty* (see page 13) a finger after it has played, then shift weight to the next one, and so on.

Descending Slurs—#5

GOALS:
1. Start from a *ready position* where both fingers are on the string,
   but not pressing.
2. Pull off quickly into the fingerboard, "snapping" the string off the fingertip.

#5

Continue with:

Triplets—#6

These are important. In fact, if you only have time for one left-hand exercise, *do this one*!

#6

Continue with:

Fixed-Finger Exercises—#7 & #8

GOALS:

1. Anchor the fixed fingers into the fingerboard with weight (try not to press).
2. Keep the moving fingers light like feathers.
3. While exchanging fingers 3 and 4, it's alright to pivot slightly, but otherwise only move the fingers themselves.

#7

#8

Right-Hand Walking — #9

GOALS:
1. For warming up, use rest strokes.
2. "Bounce" back immediately to the next note.
3. Project (dig in and get a good volume!).
4. *Always* strive for good tone.
5. Making up your own versions or variations to suit your own needs is encouraged!

#9

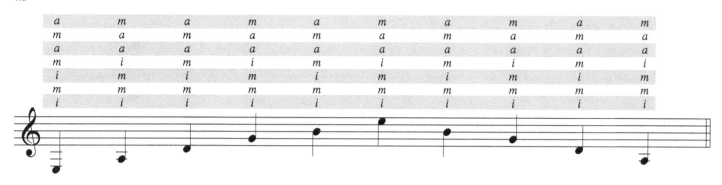

Some rhythmic variations:

Two-Finger Rasgueados — #10

GOALS:
1. Anchor the right thumb on the fourth string.
2. Attack the strings from slightly above using the backs of the fingernails.
3. Sound all three strings at once by snapping quickly through the strings, rather than strumming.

#10

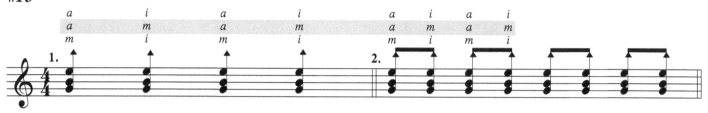

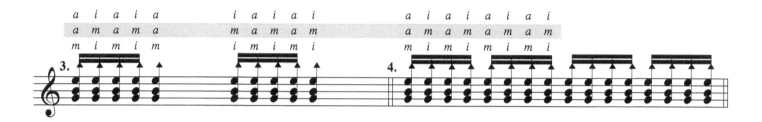

*"Those who cannot feel the littleness of
great things in themselves
are apt to overlook the greatness of
little things in others."*

• "The Book of Tea" by Okakura Kakuzō •

TREMOLO

Judging from the frustrated attitudes I have encountered on the subject, tremolo is certainly one of the most challenging of techniques. Difficult and frustrating it may be, but I believe we are fortunate as guitarists to call it our own. It isn't tremolo that is unique to our instrument, but the way we do it. It is an illusion we create—an illusion in which the melody seems to be constantly sustained, although it is not.

The key to success in playing a good tremolo is not speed, as most students believe, but evenness of articulation. The more articulate each note, the faster the tremolo seems. The more articulate the tremolo, the more control we have over it.

Psychological Outlook

Strive for control rather than speed. Learn to think of your thumb as just another finger. One of the problems many players have with tremolo is that they think of their thumb as a heavier, more forceful appendage. This leaves them with the psychological burden of *fitting in* the other three notes between thumb strokes. Instead of dividing tremolo into *one* + *three* notes (thumb plus the three fingers), these individuals should think of it as simply *four* notes played by four consecutive fingers.

Let's try to put this into practice. Before you play Exercise #1, just play steady eighth notes on one string, using, of course, *p-a-m-i*. Play them at a slow tempo. Listen very carefully to make sure they sound even—are they all the same volume and of the same length? This is an important preliminary exercise for tremolo, because eventually you will rely on your ears to play your tremolo for you; you will hear an inaccuracy, and your fingers will automatically adjust. Get used to listening well instead of just watching your fingers.

Exercises

Exercises 1–3
Keep the notes short throughout your tremolo practice, not just in this exercise. I have found that practicing a slower tremolo staccato makes it sound extremely smooth when played quickly. It also feels easier to play quickly after having practiced it in this way slowly.

In this exercise we are gradually incorporating *speed bursts*. When doing speed bursts of any kind, it is essential that one always returns immediately to the slower note values. This gives us a reference point; and, eventually—when the length of the burst increases—the faster version should feel no different than the slow one. Playing all the notes staccato for now enables us to hear the length and volume of each note more clearly, and as long as we can hear it, we can control it.

GOALS:
1. Practice each one until the fast notes feel easy.
2. Do not move on until the first one feels easy.
3. Strive for equal volume on all notes.
4. Strive for equal duration on all notes.
5. *Feel* each note *before* you play it.
6. *Listen* to each *as* you play it!

Exercise 4

This exercise involves moving the thumb from string to string. It is very important to gain control of the thumb. Place it accurately and make direct movements. You may want to incorporate the idea of alternating slower notes with faster bursts in this exercise. Don't ignore the thumb tone!

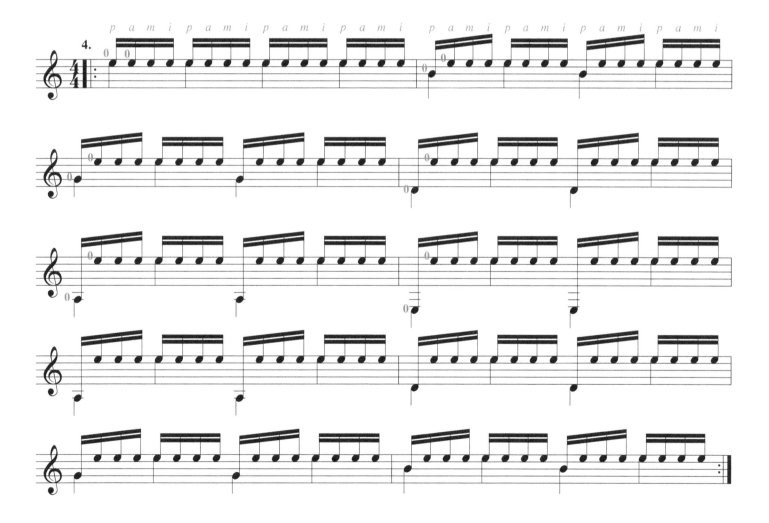

Exercises 5–10

Here are some different ways to practice tremolo. Each one accomplishes something slightly different. Adding accents is beneficial for an uneven tremolo; just listen to yourself and pinpoint what note is weaker than the others, and accent that note. The accent is not put there to make the note louder, necessarily, but to insure that you **feel** that note more intensely. Accenting it without feeling the note is empty practice.

Numbers 8 and 9 are two different types of tremolo used by flamenco guitarists, and each should be mastered.

Number 10 is my favorite overall remedy for a sloppy, weak, or uneven tremolo: a backwards tremolo. Try it!

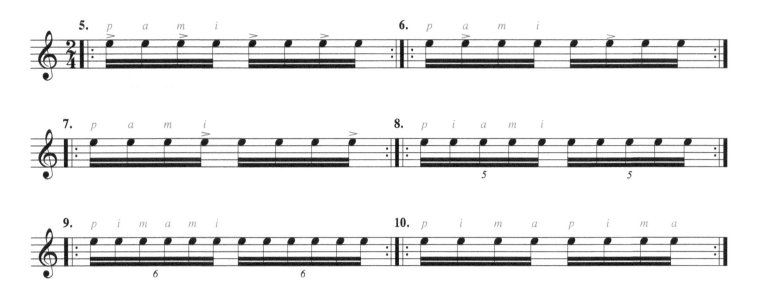

Exercise 11

Learning to change the tremolo pattern as illustrated in Exercise 11 is a very useful tool for getting control over this technique. This kind of practice is especially useful when applied to an actual piece of music, such as *Recuerdos de la Alhambra, Campanas del Alba*, or whatever tremolo piece you are currently trying to smooth out.

Lopsided Tremolos

The examples that follow are certainly good for anyone to practice, but are primarily designed to help correct "lopsided" tremolos. A lopsided tremolo is one that has too much of a gap between either *p* and *a*, or between *i* and *p*.

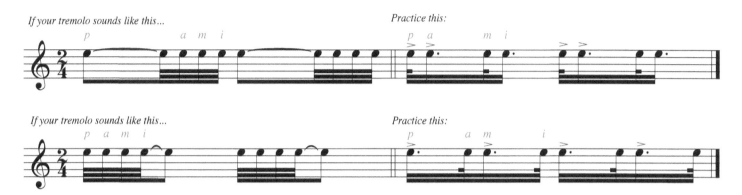

"Chant" by Brian Head: A Tremolo Study

This piece is directly inspired by the composer's orchestral composition of the same name. It is unique in that the notes often change in the middle of the tremolo pattern, thus creating a constantly fluid, moving line. Take note of the following:

1. Make sure that the right and left hands are well synchronized for the moving notes within the tremolo patterns.

2. Even though the ideal tempo lies between ♩=130–140, start as slow as 60 while learning the piece.

3. Strive for clarity rather than speed. A well-defined tremolo and a slightly slower tempo (if necessary) will best enhance the mood of the piece.

You will have better success if you first practice the preparatory exercises on the next page, which are taken from the right hand patterns and left hand movements from the piece. Get comfortable with each one before moving on.

(score begins on page 90)

"Chant" Preparation

No. 1

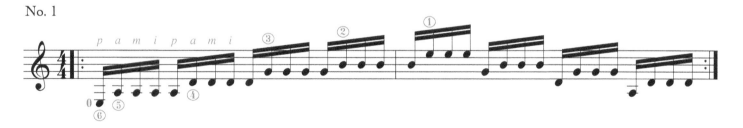

No. 2

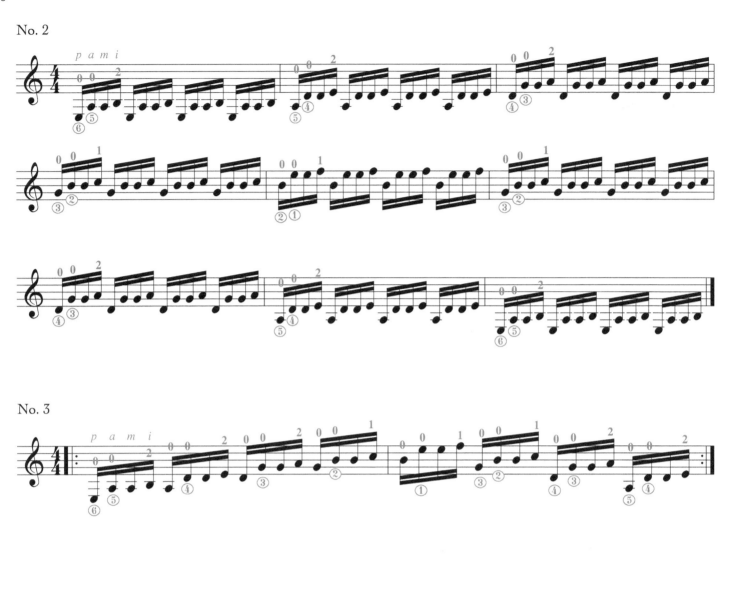

No. 3

No. 4

"To climb steep hills requires slow pace at first."

• William Shakespeare •

Chant

Track 7

Brian Head

SCALES: CONTROL AND VELOCITY

Control is more important than speed. If you can exercise control while playing, speed will follow easily when necessary. There are several general misconceptions about speed, especially in scales:

Misconceptions about speed...

1. *Without a certain amount of speed one is not a good player.* The fastest players are not necessarily the best players.
2. *Speed is a goal—rather than a tool.* Speed is something we use towards a musical end.
3. *One must be able to play very fast for long stretches of time.* Many students fail to recognize that the vast majority of scale passages in the repertoire requiring speed are only one or two measures long.

There are four elements to be mastered for the development of scale speed. They are:

1. Right-hand velocity.
2. Synchronization of the right and left hands.
3. String crossing.
4. Piecing together.

Each element shall be addressed briefly, along with an exercise.

Right-Hand Velocity

Right-hand velocity refers to how well you're able to pluck a series of notes in rapid succession with your right hand. Towards this end, practice *speed bursts*. A *speed burst* is a long string of slow notes interrupted by a short burst of fast notes. At first, you should frequently return to the slow notes between bursts; the slower notes act as a launching pad for the quick ones.

Here are a series of speed-burst exercises. Make sure each exercise is secure before moving on to the next one. While they're new to you, practice them using rest stroke, being strict about the staccato markings. After that feels good, try playing them using a legato free stroke.

1.

2.

3.

4.

5.

6.

7.

96

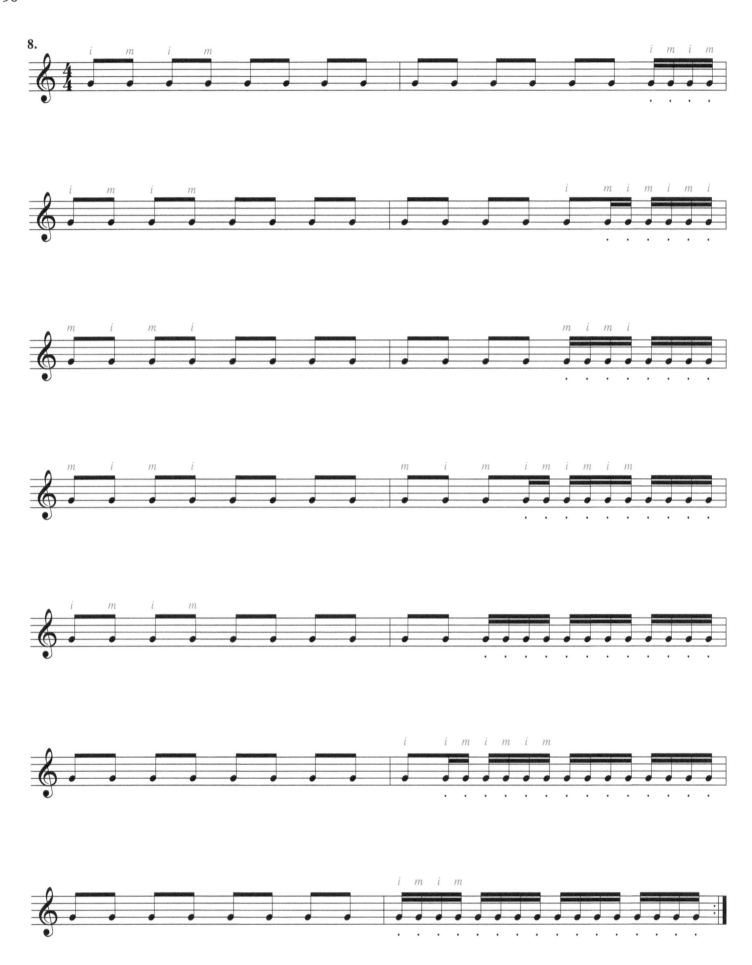

Synchronization

Synchronization means playing the right-hand finger at the exact same time as the left-hand finger. In the exercise that follows, set your tempo with the sixteenth notes in mind. Play as slowly as necessary to remain in control of the sixteenth notes. Push yourself to faster tempos a little at a time. When a passage feels good and in control at a given tempo, turn the metronome up just one notch or two until you reach the desired speed.

String Crossing

A good deal has already been said about string crossing. It is covered in the "Right-Hand Finger Independence" section on page 65. The exercises presented there are the best ones on which to focus for improving finger accuracy and speed during crossing strings. Also, see the section about marking string crossings on page 103.

Piecing Things Together

Assuming you've been working on your string crossing, the speed bursts are now comfortably speedy, and your hands are synchronized, the most logical thing to do now is to put everything together.

The easiest skill to acquire in the realm of speed is playing fast on one string. The situation that slows us down considerably is having to switch strings. Familiarize yourself with the next little exercise, but don't stop there. Work out all your most difficult scales the same way.

Here is a chromatic scale in groups of three. This is my favorite exercise for working up speed. I particularly like to push this one up one metronome notch at a time. For technical focus, though, *make sure your hands are synchronized!*

Some Other Speed Aids

Here is a chromatic scale with some rhythmic variations. Practicing scales with various rhythmic variations is invaluable to making them faster and cleaner. Notice that certain rhythmic configurations, including dots, triplets, etc., create short speed burst situations. The variations below are just a few possibilities. Practice them with this chromatic scale fingering. You should apply them to your other scales, as well.

Rhythmic Variations

And now, for more fun, try these! Group #1 concentrates on one string, Group #2 on two strings, and in Group #3... anything goes! Remember, you can only go as fast as you can play the sixteenth notes, so work these out slowly. To reap the maximum benefits from these, think before you play every note, and feel each note as you play it.

"*Sometimes your joy is the source of your smile, but sometimes your smile can be the source of your joy*"

• Thich Nhat Hanh •

Problem Solving in Scales

Everyone is eventually confronted with scales that at first glance seem impossible to play. There is no barrier, though, that cannot be broken down and overcome.

These techniques always work for me, so there is no reason why they should not work for you, too. Basically, I do three things when I want to solve scale problems. They are:

1. Marking the right-hand string crossings (especially the awkward ones).
2. Breaking the scale down into smaller groups (in the case of a longer scale).
3. Using a guide finger in the right hand.

Marking String Crossings

Marking the string crossings refers to knowing when the string changes occur in a scale, and which fingers are crossing. In an ascending scale, *i* to *m* would be best, and *m* to *i* would be more awkward. For instance, when changing from the third to the second strings, it is easiest to change from *i* to *m*. In a descending scale, *m* to *i* is best, and *i* to *m* would be the awkward crossing. For instance, when crossing from the second to the third strings, changing from *m* to *i* is best. So, by marking the string crossings, you are just alerting yourself to exactly what your fingers need to do.

This can be done with the best results by practicing the scale with the right hand alone on open strings, as shown in the following example using the scale from Sor's famous *Opus 9 Variations*:

The scale:

The same scale
on open strings:

The example that follows shows how a much longer scale can be broken down. The original, #1, is unmeasured and contains 23 notes. In #2 it is taken at a very slow and even pace to get a good feeling for the right-hand fingering, and its open-string pattern is exposed. Exercises #3 and #4 show that when played slowly, it breaks down into groups of four, and accents are added to enable the guide finger (in this case, *i*) to mark every group of four. The guide finger is usually the strongest of the two alternating fingers, and is used to help ease the burden of alternation when we play faster. As we increase the speed, it becomes impossible to think *i-m-i-m-i-m-i-m*, so with *i* as the guide finger, we can now feel *i-i-i-i-i-i-i-i*, and simply let *m* fall in its place. In #5, groups of four notes are added on until we arrive at the whole scale. Since the accents are for technical practice, they are finally taken away.

Evolution of a Scale

from *"Tiento Antiguo"* by Joaquin Rodrigo

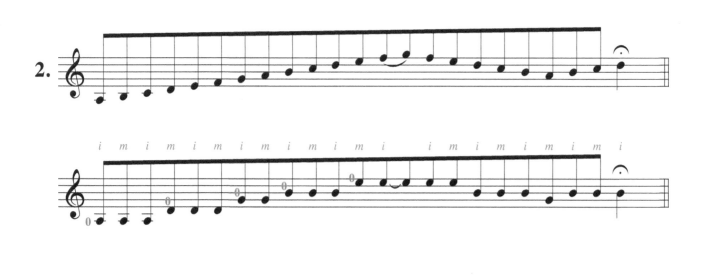

4.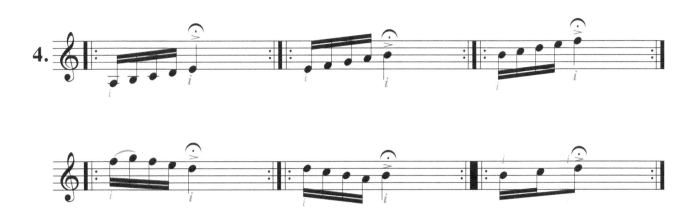

5.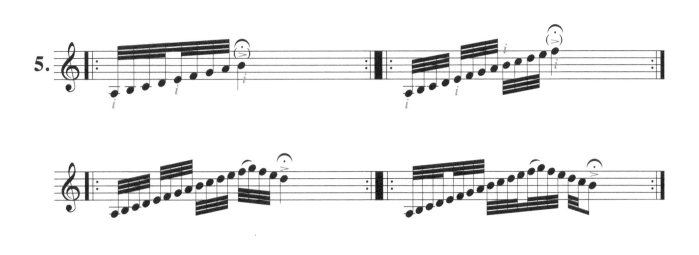

6.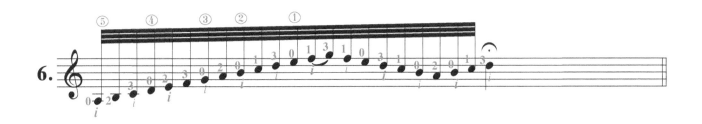

Scale Study—*Double* from the *Courante, Partita No. 1*, BWV 1002, Johann Sebastian Bach

This is the *Double* to the *Courante* from Johann Sebastian Bach's *Partita No. 1* (originally in B Minor) for solo violin, BWV 1002. This excerpt is from an arrangement in A Minor I did some time ago. I've also done it in B Minor, but I just liked the sound of it better in A Minor. When I was taking fragments from this movement to practice I discovered it makes an incredible scale study.

I have removed the bass notes that were in the original transcription and changed much of the right and left hand fingering accordingly to further focus the attention on the scales. Some of the cross-string leaps may seem unpleasant at first, but after all, it *is* a study. The bulk of the alternation is between *i* and *m*; however, all the fingerings are only suggestions. I personally use a light rest stroke throughout most of the piece, except on the notes surrounding a bass note played with the thumb. I would suggest practicing as much of it as possible with rest strokes for technical purposes, but with free strokes for musical and stylistic reasons.

Double

J. S. Bach

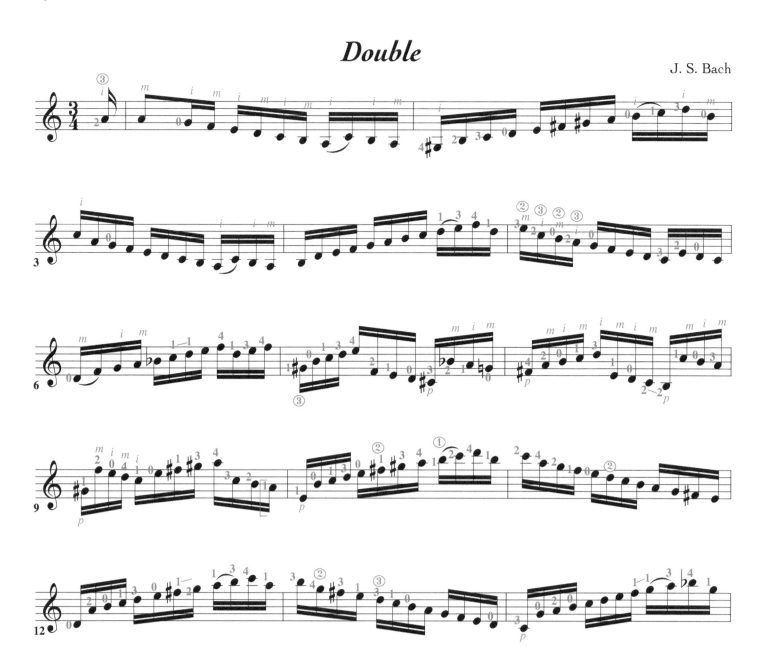

(continued)

ARPEGGIOS

A few explanations are necessary before you begin to study the arpeggio patterns covered in this section.

Full Planting and Sequential Planting

There are two ways of preparing the fingers on the strings that facilitate the playing of arpeggios. *Full planting* means that all the fingers involved in an arpeggio (excluding the thumb after the pattern has begun) are planted simultaneously. This is almost exclusively done in ascending arpeggios. *Sequential planting* involves planting the fingers one at a time, as needed (including the thumb), and is applied to descending arpeggios, and, in practice, most others as well.

Full Plant: Before playing, *p-i-m-a* are placed on the strings. After *a* plays, *p* is planted; after *p* plays, *i-m-a* are planted, and so on.

Sequential Plant: Plant *p*; after it plays, plant *a*; after it plays, plant *m*; after it plays, immediately plant *i*; after it plays, plant *p*, and so on.

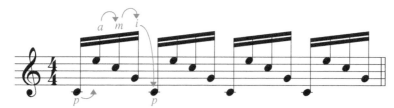

Combining full and sequential planting: In an arpeggio that ascends and descends, use a full plant on the ascending portion of the arpeggio, and plant sequentially on the descending portion.
The full plant is most widely used as a training tool for keeping the fingers close to the strings. Since

putting all the fingers down at once stops the sound momentarily, it is musically desirable to omit the full plant in many cases. For example, in Matteo Carcassi's *Etude No. 3, Opus 60*, the tempo is so leisurely that employing a full plant on the ascending arpeggio would stop everything from ringing, so using a sequential plant in this piece would be best. But it is invaluable in other situations. For instance, in the fast arpeggio section in *Leyenda*, by Albéniz, using a full plant not only aids the fingers in approaching the necessary speed, but makes the arpeggios sound crisp and articulate.

Giuliani's *120 Right-Hand Studies*

In the *120 Right-Hand Studies*, by Mauro Giuliani, both full planting and sequential planting are put to use. I have organized them into ten groups. Over the years, many students have asked me how they should practice these. I have always broken them down into groups so I am presenting them that way here. I have also put them into what I consider to be a more logical order for study.

There has been hesitation on the part of teachers to have their students practice these studies, and for two good reasons. First of all, to have 120 arpeggio studies staring at you from the music stand is a little overwhelming. Where does one begin?! Also, listening to a V–I cadence (the C to G7 chords) over a prolonged period is "cruel and unusual punishment." These two reasons aside, this group of studies is the best and most comprehensive collection of arpeggio formulas I have seen; and, having practiced all of them diligently myself, I know they deliver results!

The order of the studies has been changed. They have been grouped by each arpeggio formula and its variations. Groups 8 and 9 are exceptions, since it appears that Giuliani threw in some extra arpeggios which do not fit with any of the other formulas. Giuliani declared that if one could play all of these studies well, one could successfully play anything he ever wrote. You know, I think I believe him!

Practicing Tips

My first piece of advice to you is to not ignore the very first study. Although it is comprised of just block chords, it functions well at the beginning to help balance the hand. Listen for perfect balance between the voices as you play it, and make sure your strokes and releases are quick and powerful.

Take one group at a time to practice; not necessarily all in one session, but take your time and feel secure with each before moving on to the next. If one or more patterns in a group are naturally easy for you, bypass them in favor of those that are difficult. Also, feel free to play different chords, or even open strings, as long as the patterns stay the same.

In a short time, after you have practiced them all you will, no doubt, have compiled a mental list of the ones that give you problems. Work on those daily. You can also select one from each group, and practice the studies in that way. Go ahead—get started!

112

Group #1

Group #2

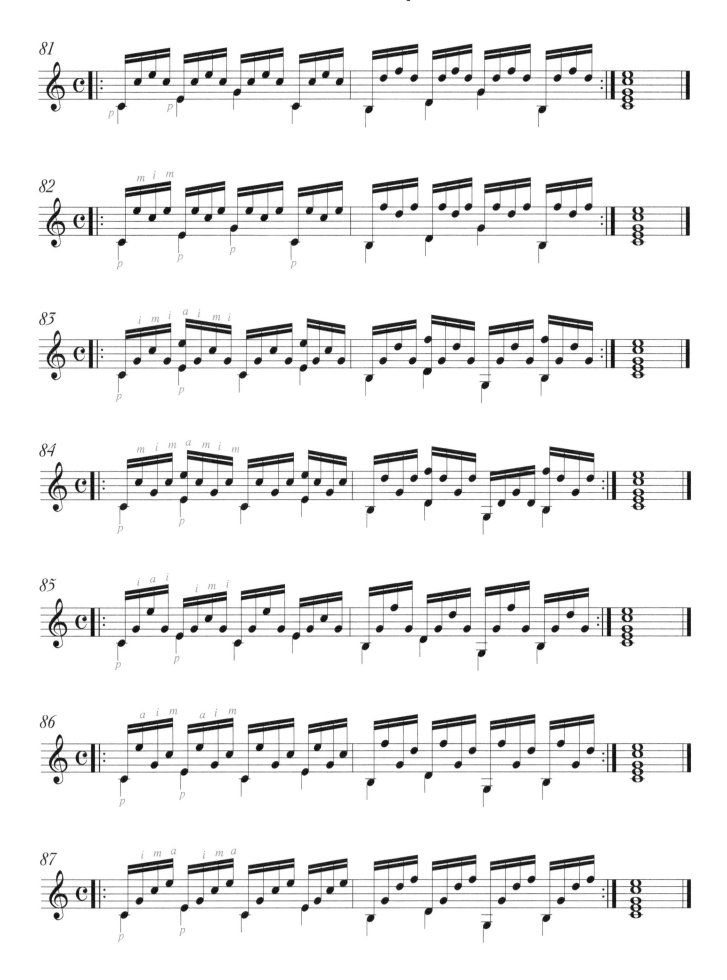

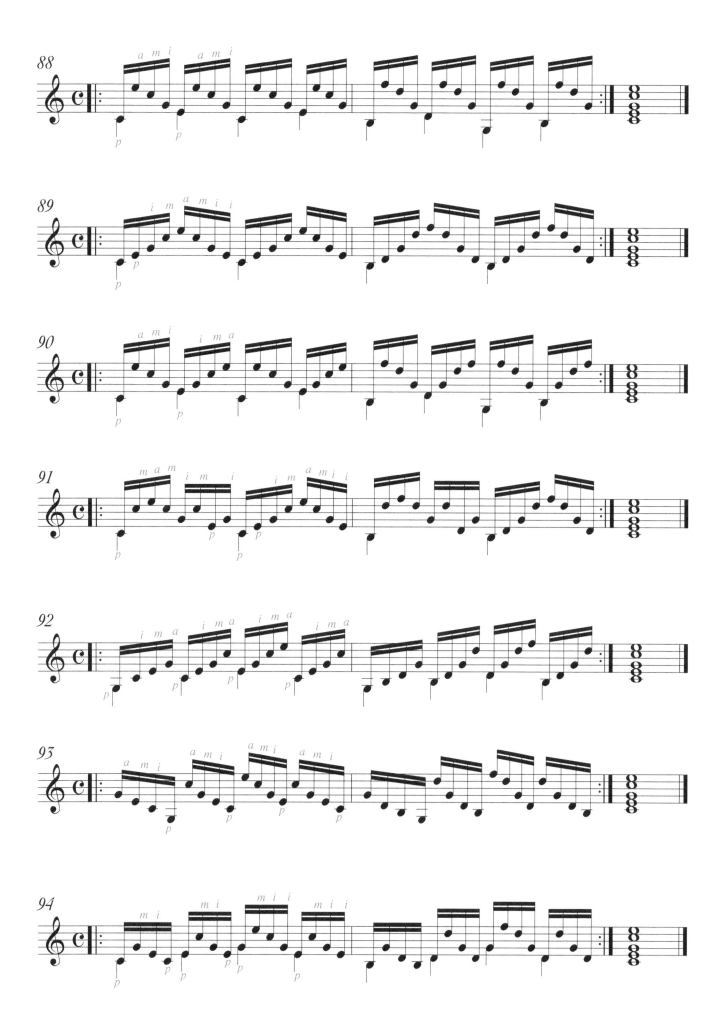

Group #3

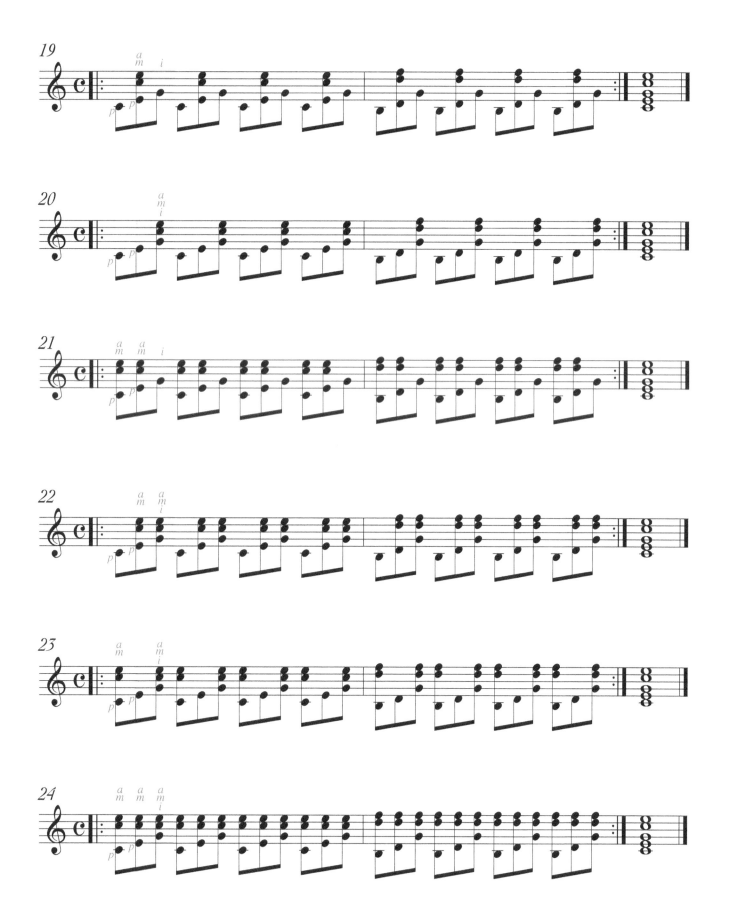

118

Group #4

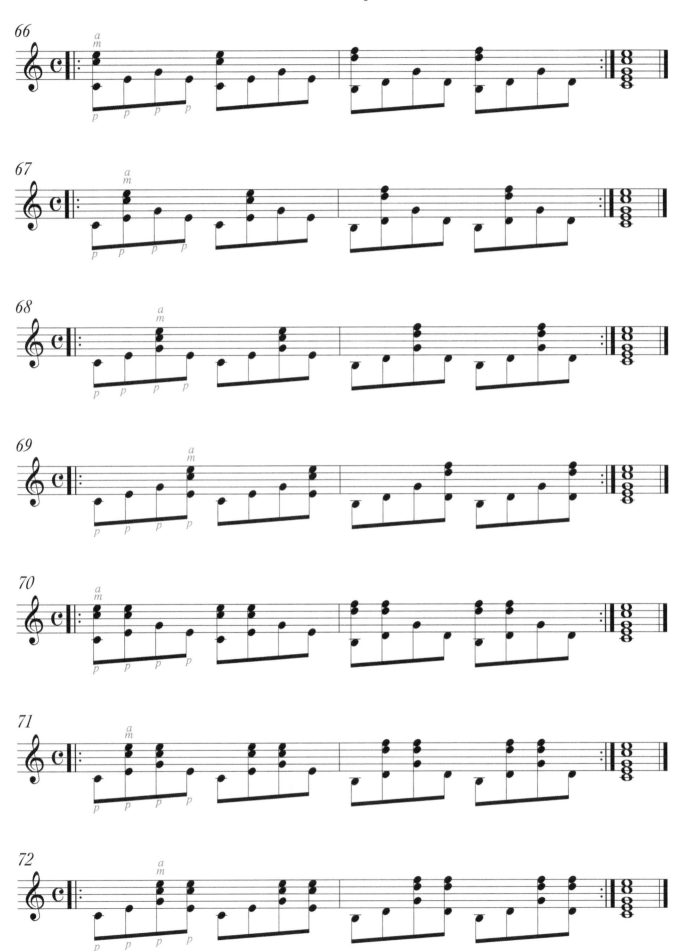

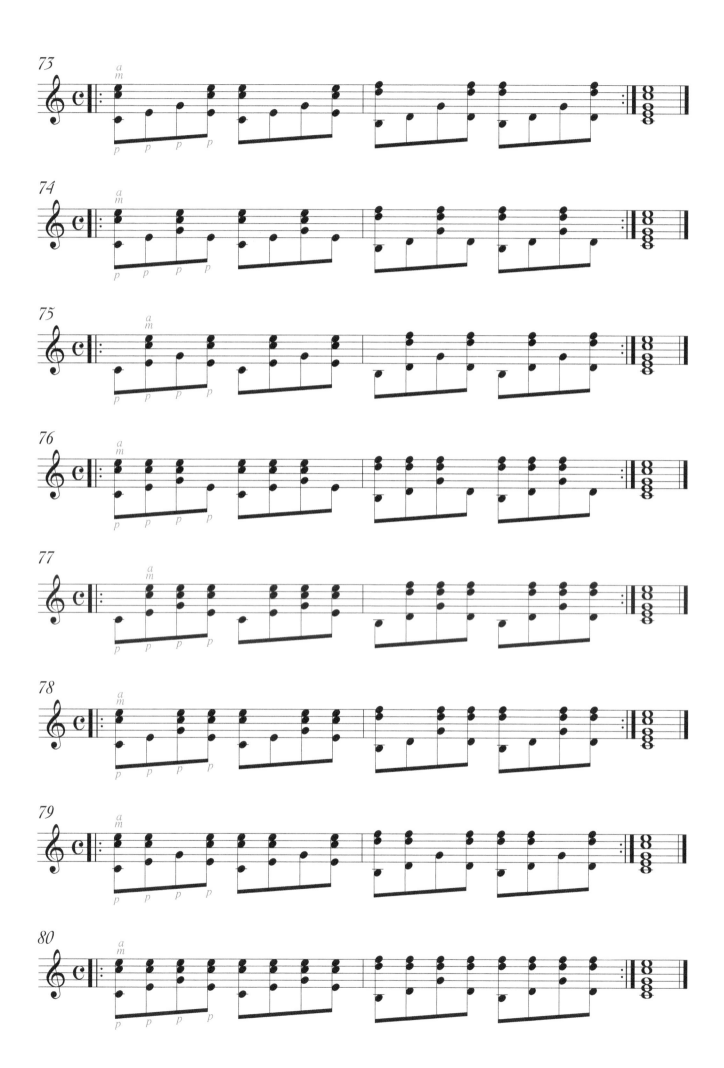

Group #5

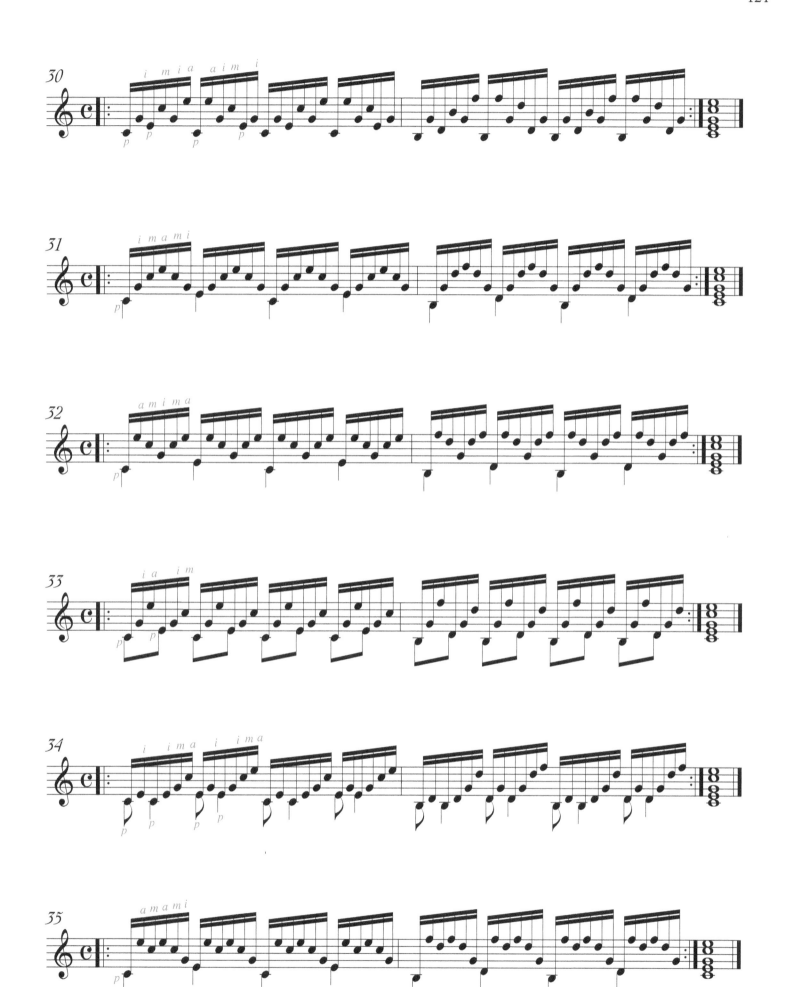

122

Group #6

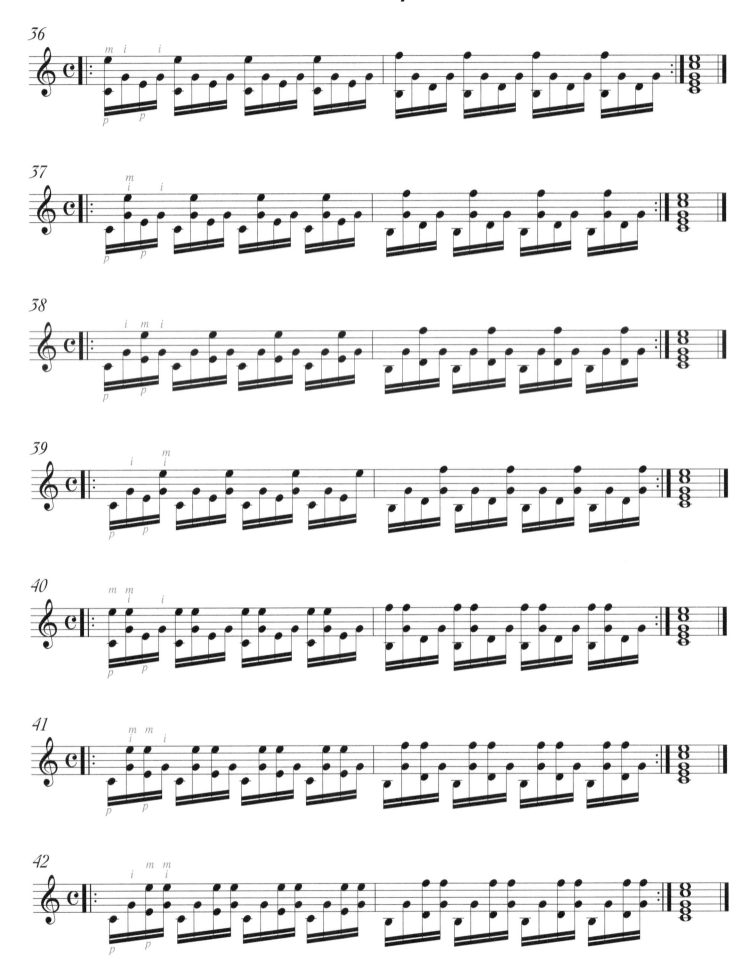

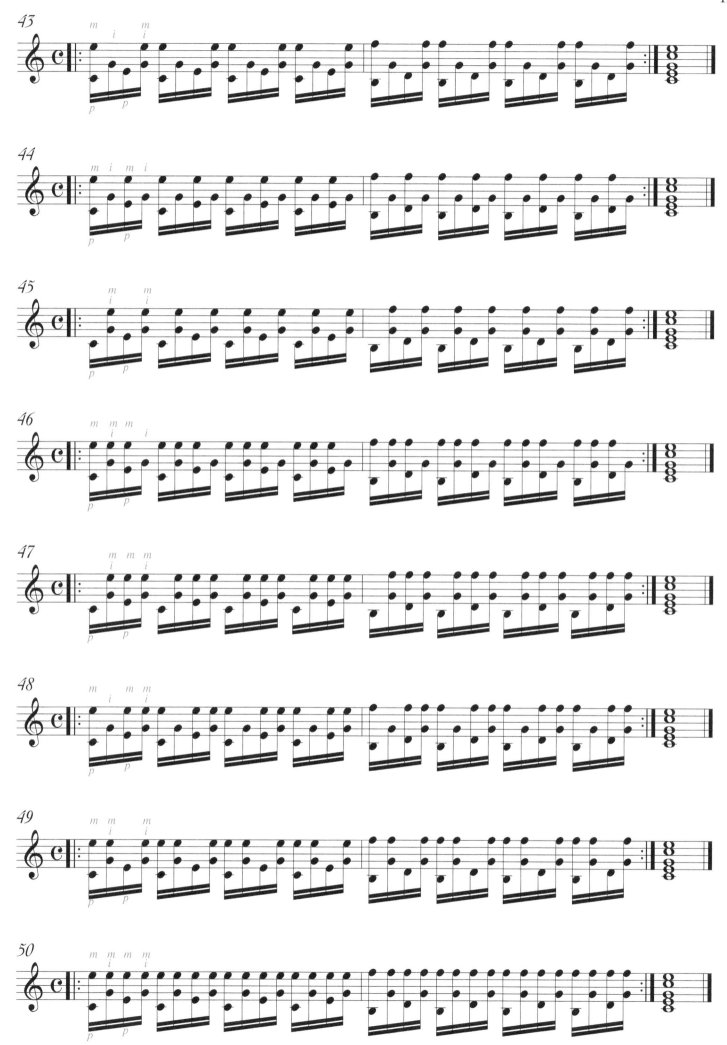

Group #7

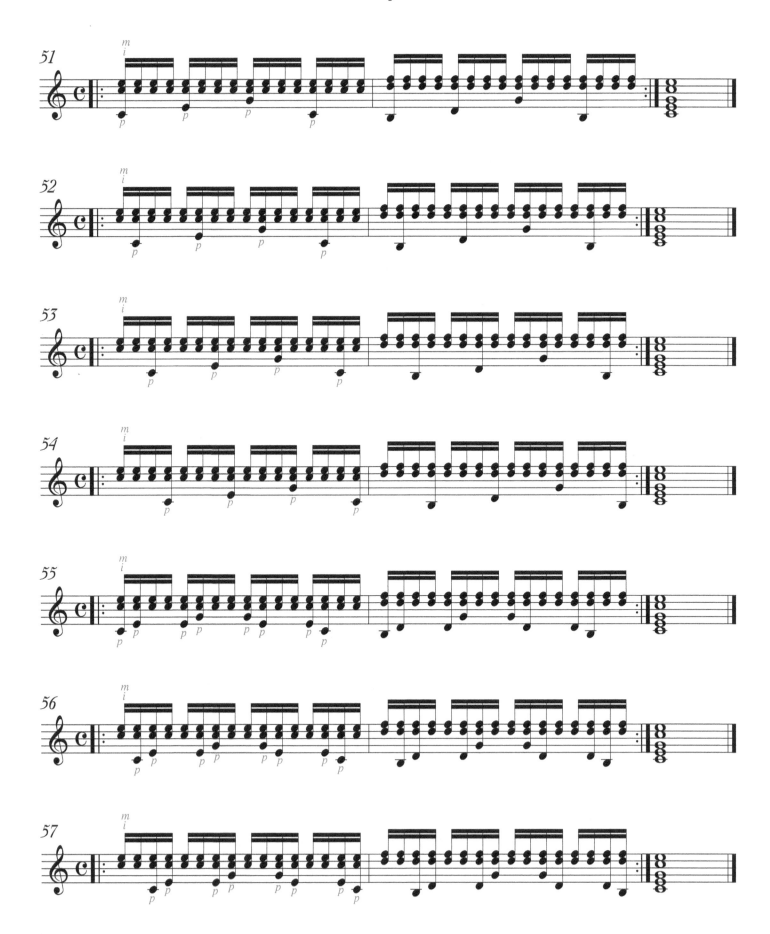

Group #8

128

Group #9

Group #10

"Shapeshifting," An Arpeggio Etude
by Evan Hirschelman

"Shapeshifting" was written as an arpeggio etude, and is the second movement of a two-movement work (the first movement is a harmonics etude). This work employs numerous right-hand fingering variations, many of which can be found in the ubiquitous Right-Hand Studies, Opus 1, by Mauro Giuliani. It is my hope that this work offers additional avenues for expanding your arpeggio technique, while also increasing stamina and musicality in the process. The minimalistic qualities of this work should allow the performer to not only strive for cleanliness in their technique, but also emphasize timbral and musical nuance in their interpretation, bringing more dimension to the composition.

–Evan Hirschelman

Please pay attention to:

- Any transition with a changing arpeggio pattern (e.g., measures 9–10, 12, 25, 31, etc.)

- The transition of straight 16th-note arpeggios to sextuplet patterns should flow without any disruption in the rhythmic texture. The changing arpeggio patterns should sound somewhat imperceptible in timbre and rhythmic flow. These transitions should sound seamless, unless they are dynamically notated differently.

- The accented notes (e.g., page 133) should be performed dynamically, and adjusted relative to the general phrasing.

- Measure 93 has a barre, followed by a hinge-barre during the eighth-note rest, which allows the F♯ in the bass to ring through.

- At the end, the last harmonic note requires the 1st finger to hold the B-note, while the 4th finger simultaneously plays the F♯ (above the 5th fret).

Shapeshifting
Track 8
II.

Evan Hirschelman

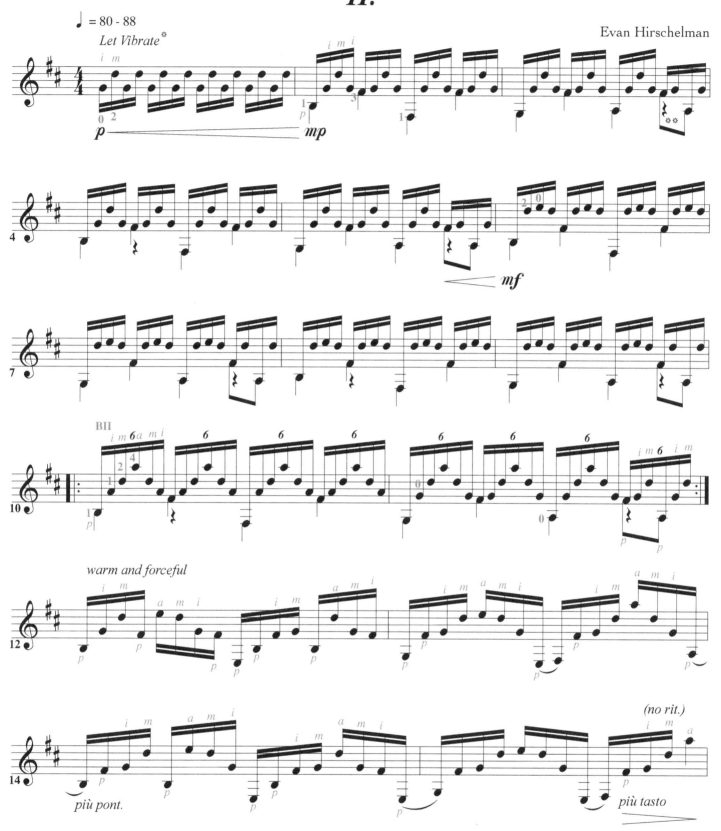

* Let all notes vibrate, except 5th & 6th string melody notes (stems down). These melody
notes should not ring through each other. In addtion, 5th string melody notes that are
followed by a rest are dampened by lifting or using the backside of thumb.

** With this rest, the composer is emphasizing that the previous bass note should be stopped.

NOTE: The dynamic qualities of accented notes
should change according to phrasing

136

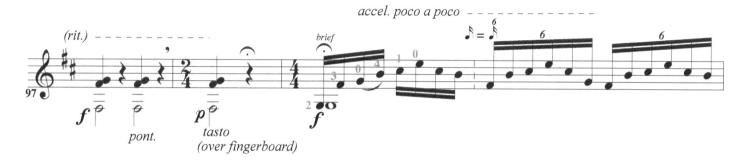

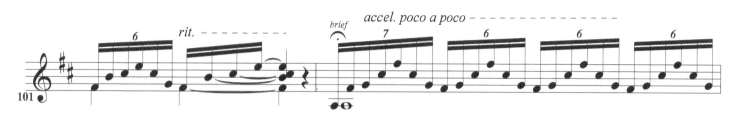

* 1st finger holds B note, 4th finger produces F♯ harmonic, slightly above the 5th fret on ⑤.

"All the good music has already been written by people with wigs and stuff"

• Frank Zappa •

Didactic Doodle by Andrew York

Here is an arpeggio piece that will give anyone a run for their money! Thus far in the arpeggio section of this book, there have been plenty of opportunities to practice a particular pattern over and over again. Andy's *Didactic Doodle* deliberately strings together several challenging arpeggio patterns, none of them lasting for more than a few bars.

Here are some important things to remember:

1. Work on each pattern by itself, first:
   Pattern 1—measures 1 and 2 (5 and 6)
   Pattern 2—measure 7
   Pattern 3—measure 8
   Pattern 4—measure 9
   Pattern 5—measure 10
   Pattern 6—measures 12 and 13
   Pattern 7—measure 15
   Pattern 8—measures 16, 18 and 20
   Pattern 9—measures 17, 19 and 21
   Pattern 10—measures 22 and 23
   Pattern 11—measures 25, 26, 27, and 28

2. Piece them together gradually.

3. Work the accents into the patterns as you practice them individually.

140

Didactic Doodle

Track 9

Andrew York

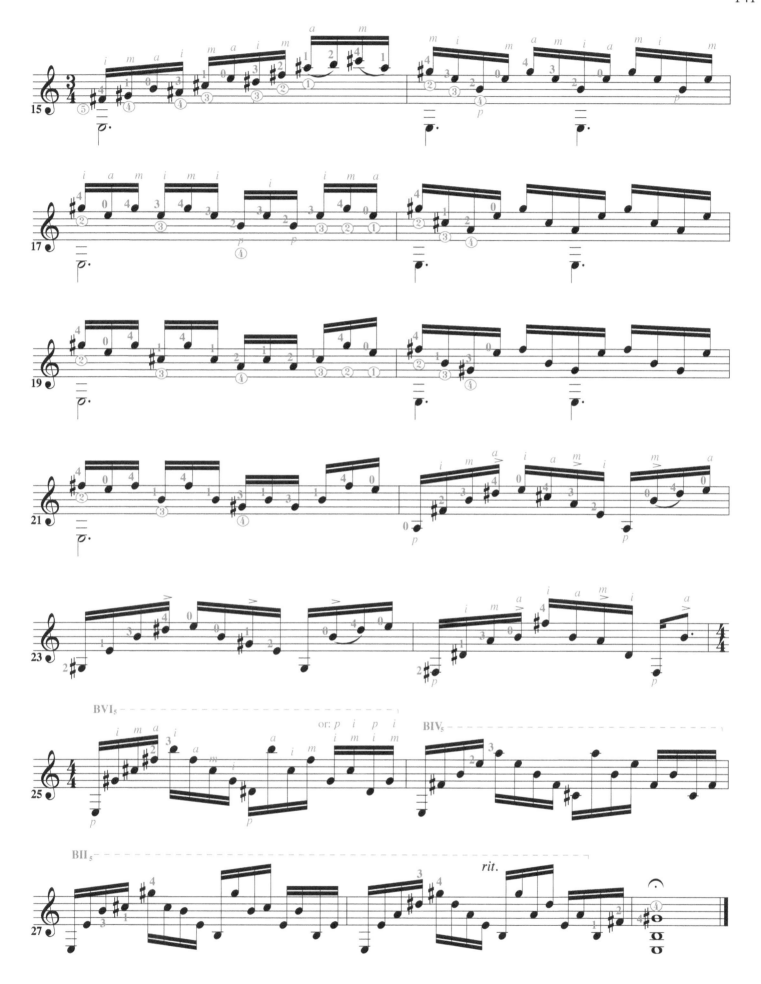

AFTERWORD

Performance Anxiety

There is no substitute for preparation. Being well prepared for a performance gives us the confidence and the self-assurance we need to "go on with the show." However, no matter how well we prepare in advance, there is always that last-minute anxiety from the feeling that we didn't do enough. I think we've all felt this at one time or another, and probably practiced and played the instrument all day the day of the concert, only to feel tired, more insecure, and even more nervous than before! As a result of a tough situation I found a solution for myself that may work for you, too.

It happened when I had to give two concerts for the same organization. The first one was in the evening and the second one was the next afternoon. The entire day before the first performance I had absolutely nothing scheduled, and decided I would just take my time and go slowly through the entire program. I thought I was using my time wisely, but as I practiced, I found little things in the music were giving me problems which had not bothered me before. OH NO!!! My mental composure continued on a downward slide the rest of the day. By the time I settled in for my pre-concert nap I was a mess! Needless to say, I napped not. At the concert that night, I had several memory slips, among some other small problems. With my self-confidence shattered, I awaited the next day's recital.

The following day I arose late and had little time for breakfast. Since the concert was out in the country somewhere, my hosts informed me we would leave right away to allow plenty of time. It was just time enough, because we arrived at the venue only ten minutes before the downbeat. I sat up my things on the stage, went back and tuned up, and rushed out on stage and played one of my best concerts ever!

The lesson: not only did I not have time that day to play, warm up, or even think about the concert, I also *didn't have time to worry about it*. Nowadays I actually play the guitar very little the day of a concert. I'll just tune up that morning, make sure my strings sound alright, and touch-up my nails if they need it. I try to stay in a normal and "happy" frame of mind. If I'm not happy, I find a way to make myself happy. I'll read, watch something funny on TV, think of things I like doing, go for a walk, call someone on the phone; or anything else that seems like it will do the trick. I try to take a short nap (just fifteen to thirty minutes or so) before I leave for the concert . This clears my head. Backstage, just before the concert, I remind myself of a few things:

1. I think, "This is great! I can't wait to play!" After all, this is what I've wanted to do all my life.
2. I think of what the program is; or better still, I like to have one in front of me to review while I warm up.
3. I warm up with light exercises only: stretches, short scales, and/or selections from the Daily Warm-Up Routine in this book. I don't "run through" anything.
4. I let myself feel my nervousness and don't try to get rid of my nerves anymore, or "freak out" when I am nervous. I just expect to be nervous. As with the airline attendants who endlessly hassle me about taking my guitar on board, I have learned to confront nerves on their terms and with confidence. By feeling my nervousness, I'm accepting the fact that I am nervous; but acknowledge only the physical signs, such as a fast heart rate, sweating, lack of sufficient oxygen or even nausea. I focus on each one individually for a few seconds. Some form of steady deep breathing (see description next page) almost always helps these symptoms subside. I refuse to let them conquer me. Unlike the airline attendants, most of the nerves eventually go away! I convert the remaining nerves into excitement about playing the concert. I think to myself, "No more endless repetitions of these pieces; all I have to do is run everything once and that's it! How easy!"

I like to remind myself of something my teacher, Pepe Romero, told me when I was 14: "No matter what, the sun always comes out the next day and life goes on." After all, the troubles didn't matter at all, and somebody most certainly walked out of the concert happier than before!

5.   Then, I go out on stage and just go for it. I let my "inner player" play the concert for me; that player we all have inside us which usually emerges when we're playing in front of the TV watching old *Star Trek* re-runs or the NCAA playoffs!

Also don't forget that without being nervous we produce very little adrenaline. Playing a concert without being at least a little nervous makes for a lackluster performance.

A Simple Deep Breathing Routine
Inhale deeply and observe how you feel as you hold your breath. Then, fully and slowly exhale while expelling your nerves out with the breath.

Practice

Always practice with a purpose. Practicing without a purpose is like a broken pencil: pointless. Have a clear idea of what you need to practice. Organize the hierarchy of items you want to improve upon. Some are long-term (such as practicing the *Concierto de Aranjuez*) and within those long-term goals are smaller goals (such as improving your tone) that can be accomplished in one or two practice sessions.

Remember that whenever you play a note on the guitar you have two choices: to improve or go downhill. If you practice without getting anything done, you've either not concentrated hard enough or put too many things on the menu for the day. Next time, focus on smaller goals. Allowing yourself to make even a bad tone on the instrument without taking steps to correct it is not acceptable. Any chance you waste to play something well is a step downhill. There is always something on which you can improve, no matter how small, whenever you pick up the instrument. There is practice and there is playing (going for it). The common thread between the two is the simple discipline we cultivate of striving for that little glimmer of excellence.

"Whether you think you can, or you think you can't—you're right."

• Henry Ford •

Inspiration

Inspiration only lasts a relatively brief time. We all eventually find ourselves experiencing a "dry spell." We get stuck on something in our practicing and can't seem to improve, and sometimes it may seem that we're getting worse. At times we may even think of just quitting. Have you ever felt that the joy you once had for playing is gone forever?

These are not emotions you're experiencing alone. They visit everyone now and then. Occasionally we need to give ourselves a break and put down the guitar for a day, a few days, or however long it takes to feel refreshed again. For those who play for a living and don't always have that luxury, some digging back into one's past might be the key. Why did you want to play the guitar in the first place? Try to recall the feelings you experienced when you first decided that you really wanted to play. Perhaps recall the joy you felt when you heard that first recording or concert that thrilled you. What qualities about the instrument first drew you to it?

As I have done for several circumstances in my life, it may make you feel better to jot down a few of these positive thoughts on a piece of paper. Then, when you hit another rough period, you can read through them.

In Conclusion

Music is the most powerful of all the arts. It instantly stirs up emotions, conjures visions, and offers glimpses of other, higher dimensions. It arouses men to battle; kindles amorous passions in lovers; soothes a baby to sleep; comforts us when we grieve. It engages our hearts and our minds, and can bring out the best that we are. One can safely presume that not a single emotion, nor any human or natural event, has been left undocumented by music.

As musicians, our objective is to command the elements of music as best we can in order to tap into that other dimension. It is our access into heaven, if only for a while. But while we are there we can take all who are listening with us. If just one person is uplifted by our playing and walks away feeling better than before he came, we have made a difference. A healing has taken place.

I very much hope that you have found at least one thing in this book that has helped you. I also hope that, as you work to improve your technique, you do not lose sight of the larger goals: to be able to express yourself freely on your instrument and to turn every note you play into great music. When you can do those things, you cease to be just a guitar player and become a healer and magician.

COMPLETE

SECOND EDITION

PUMPING NYLON

PART 2

Easy to Early
Intermediate Repertoire

Audio tracks recorded at Penguin Studios, Pasadena, CA; mastered
at Bar None Studio, Northford, CT

CONTENTS

This table of contents is designed to help you use this section as effectively as possible. Not only will it give you an "at-a-glance" tour of what the section contains and help you find the specific piece you seek, but it will also help you find pieces that relate to the specific areas of technique you wish to study. The pieces appear in order of difficulty. The categories of technique are shown across the top. The boxes checked next to a piece tell you which technique(s) apply to that piece. The technique categories are taken directly from the first section of this book. — *Nathaniel Gunod*

PREFACE

Welcome! Are you ready to play?

The pieces in this section are selected and designed around the various techniques addressed in the first part of this book. They are offered as an extension of those exercises, and to provide attractive and easy pieces in which to apply the various techniques discussed. They come from many traditional sources as well as from some exciting contemporary composers. These pieces have helped me and my students over the years. If practiced correctly and with the proper intent, they will aid in developing your technical skills.

I originally wanted to steer clear of all of those so-called "old, boring, old-fashioned" studies that everyone (and everyone's father and grandfather) considers out-dated. We all know what they are; those nameless, numbered etudes by the previously living. But after looking around at what was available, I came to the same conclusion that other guitar teachers have repeatedly in the past: the guitarist/composers of the past had some great pedagogical ideas. Their studies were made to help solve certain technical problems that they and their students encountered; the same challenges we face today. Where this collection of etudes differs from the many others available today is that we have selected pieces that will help develop certain specific classical guitar techniques dealt with in the first section of this book. Suggestions are given to guide your practice and help you focus on the challenges at hand.

Each piece is preceded by a "checklist" of specific issues upon which to focus, such as technical and/ or musical challenges, left- and right-hand fingerings and practicing tips. Although everyone's playing levels and technical boundaries are different, these studies should be of great benefit if the checklist is taken to heart.

As always, it is a good idea to check your progress with a teacher when problems arise, as there is no ideal substitute for the real thing. I suggest you take the ideas presented in each piece and expand on them by finding other pieces that will further help you in overcoming your difficulties.

So, now, 1...2...ready...

Glossary of Signs and Terms

This list will help you to interpret the various markings in the music.

1, 2, 3, 4	Left hand fingers, numbered from index (1) to pinky (4).
p, i, m, a	Right hand fingers: *p* = thumb, *i* = index, *m* = middle, *a* = ring finger.
①②③④⑤⑥	The six strings of the guitar, numbered from low E⑥ to high E①.
IV, V, VII, etc.	Roman numerals. Used to indicate frets. Here is a quick review of these symbols: I=1, II=2, III=3, IV=4, V=5, VI=6, VII=7, VIII=8, IX=9, X=10, XI=11 and XII=12.
BII₄	The B indicates a barre. The Roman numeral indicates the fret to be barred, and the small number indicates the amount of strings to be barred. So, this symbol indicates to barre four strings at the second fret.
-1, -2, -3, -4	A dash in front of a fingering indicates a *guide finger shift*. A *shift* is a movement from one position to another. A *guide finger* is a finger that can be used just before and just after a shift. For instance, if the 4th finger has been used to play G on the 1st string, 3rd fret, and then moves to play A on the 1st string, 5th fret, it will be marked -4 .
⑥ = D	Tune the 6th string down to D.
⊕	*Coda* sign. Marks the ending section of a piece.
℅	*Segno.* When playing a D. S. al Fine form, go back to this sign and play to the end.
♩ = 60	Tempo marking. In this case, the metronome should be set to 60. Each click represents a quarter note.
♩ ⸆	*Accent.* Emphasize.
♩ ·	*Staccato.* Short. Detached.
♩ ‾	*Tenuto.* To hold a note for its full value.
a tempo	Return to the original *tempo* or speed.
Allegro	Lively, cheerful, fast.
Andante	A moderate, walking tempo.
Andantino	Slightly faster than *andante*.
cresc.	*Crescendo.* Gradually becoming louder.
decresc.	*Decrescendo.* Gradually becoming softer.
dim.	*Diminuendo.* Gradually becoming softer.
D. C. al Coda	Go back to the beginning of the piece and play to the coda indication, then skip down to the *Coda*.
D. C. al Fine	Da Capo al Fine. Go to the beginning and play until the *Fine*.
D. S. al Fine	Dal Segno al Fine. Go back to the sign ℅ and play until the *Fine*.
Fine	The end.
Moderato	In a moderate tempo.
molto	Very.
morendo	Dying away.
mosso	Moved. Agitated.
poco ritenuto	Immediately becoming a little held back or slower.
rall.	*Rallentando.* Becoming gradually slower.
rit.	*Ritardando.* Becoming gradually slower.
simile	When this word appears after a pattern has been established (fingerings, dynamics, etc.), it means to continue in this manner.
sub.	*Subito.* Suddenly.
Tranquillo	Tranquil, calm, quiet.

DYNAMIC SIGNS

p	*Piano.* Soft.
pp	*Pianissimo.* Very soft.
mp	*Mezzo piano.* Moderately soft.
f	*Forte.* Loud.
ff	*Fortissimo.* Very loud.
mf	*Mezzo forte.* Moderately loud.
fp	*Forte piano.* Strike a loud note and suddenly become soft.
sfz	*Sforzando.* A sudden strong accent.
◁	*Crescendo.* Gradually becoming louder
▷	*Decrescendo.* Gradually becoming softer.

DIFFERENT STROKES

Tennant/Gunod

  Track 10

This is a good study for right-hand scale work and training the thumb and fingers to simultaneously move in opposite directions (flexing and extending *p* while the fingers alternate).

CHECKLIST:

✔ Practice with *p* rest stroke and fingers free stroke.

✔ Practice with *p* free stroke and fingers rest stroke.

✔ Make strokes strong and quick, emptying (releasing the energy from) each finger when finished.

✔ Make sure free strokes have a quick and deep follow-through toward the palm.

WALKING

Tennant/Gunod Track 11

This study is an ideal application of the right-hand walking exercises in *Pumping Nylon* and is good for basic scale work.

CHECKLIST:

✔ Plant* fingers well during string crossings.

✔ Synchronize left- and right-hand finger movements.

✔ Practice slowly, but make the strokes fast and strong. PLAY SLOWLY—MOVE FAST.

✔ Practice in both rest stroke and free stroke.

*Prepare them on the strings just before plucking.

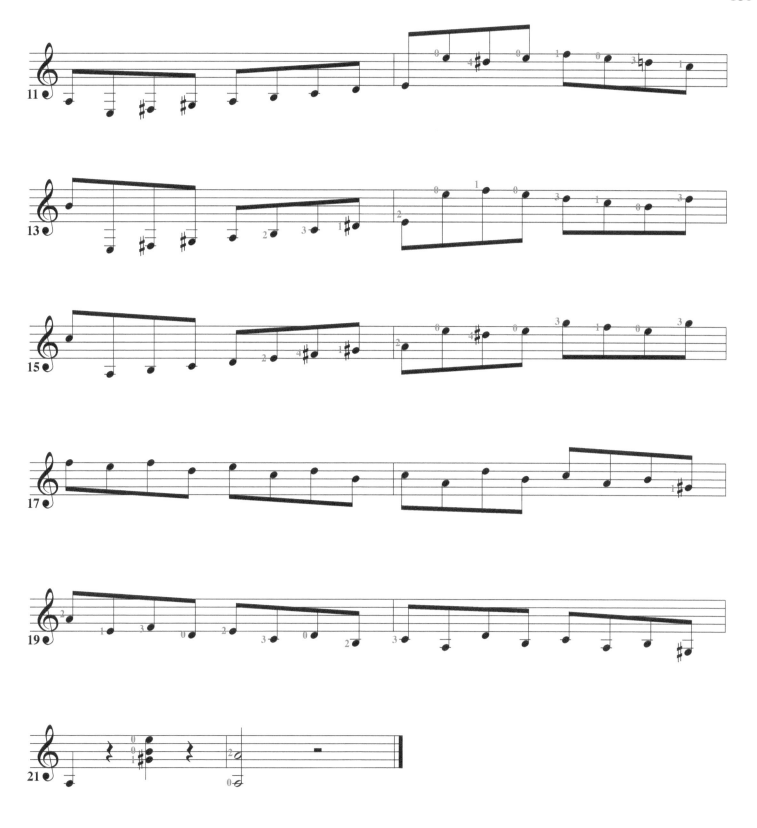

"The language of music is
understood everywhere."

• Nusrat Fateh Ali Khan •

OPUS 44, #6

Fernando Sor

Track 12

This piece includes a wide variety of techniques for you to work on.

CHECKLIST:

✔ Follow the indicated right-hand fingerings at first; later feel free to finger it comfortably for yourself.

✔ Practice *i–m* scale passages with both rest stroke and free stroke.

BIT O' NOSTALGIA

Scott Tennant Track 13

This is a good exercise for chord balancing (making all the notes in a chord sound equal) through control of right-hand finger pressure.

CHECKLIST:

✔ Listen for balance. Pay attention to the feel of the strings under the right-hand fingers and be totally aware of the amount of pressure you're applying. When you feel the string, be aware of its texture and thickness.

✔ Focus on the feel of the strings as they "give" under the pressure from the right-hand fingers.

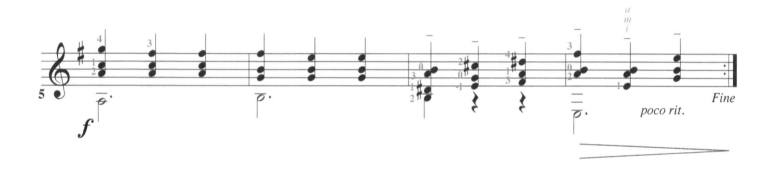

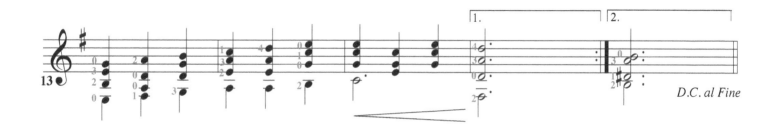

SNOWFLIGHT

Andrew York Track 14

A lovely, easy, arpeggio piece, this is one of *8 Discernments* by York.

CHECKLIST:

✔ Be very attentive to tone production.

✔ Take this opportunity to feel the independence of each right-hand finger.

✔ Don't move your left hand off of any chord before the right hand finishes the arpeggio.

✔ Follow the indicated dynamics.

155

CRISPIN'S SPIN

Omid Zoufonoun   Track 15

Aside from the obvious right-hand challenges due to its arpeggiated nature, this piece also offers some challenges for the left hand.

CHECKLIST:

✔ Don't move your left hand off of any chord before the right hand finishes the arpeggio.

✔ As with Andrew York's "Quadrivial Quandary" in *Pumping Nylon*, this piece requires the left-hand fingers to jump around quite a bit. "Visualize" ahead; look at the notes/frets on the fingerboard to which you're going and avoid staring at the chord formation you're currently playing.

✔ Change chords in a relaxed but quick manner.

ESTUDIO #2

Francisco Tarrega

Track 16

Listen closely for tone! The beautiful melody on the 1st string should have a warm, singing sound.

CHECKLIST:

✔ Play the accented notes using free stroke with *a*.

✔ Experiment with subtle differences in the a fingertip's angle to the string and the subsequent differences in tone.

✔ As with "Snowflight" and "Crispin's Spin," do not leave any chord too soon in order to get to the next one. Move from chord to chord quickly, easily and at the last moment.

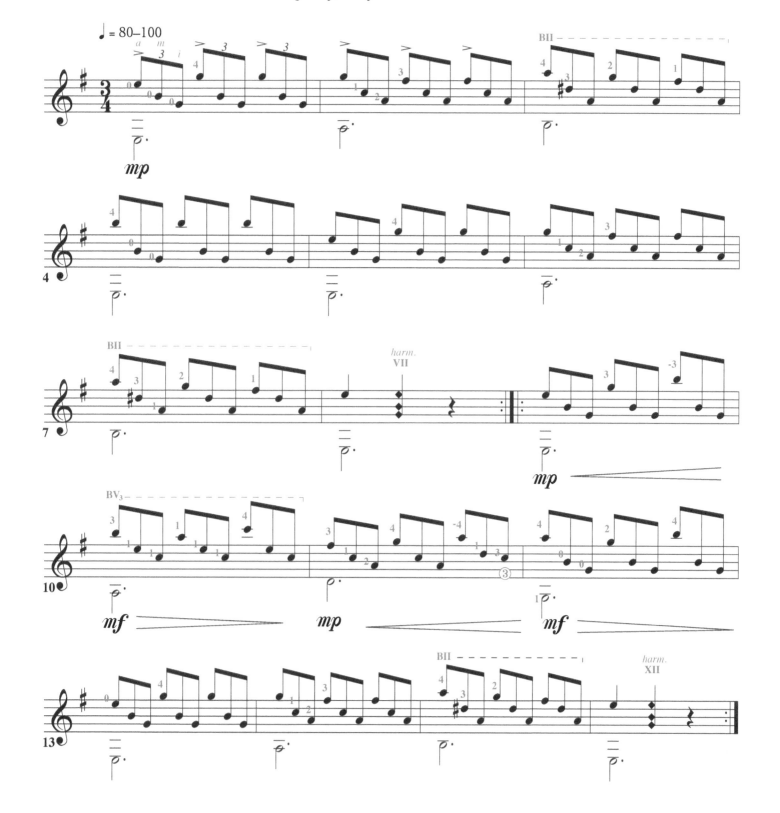

ETUDE #19

Matteo Carcassi   Track 17

This is my personal favorite of the arpeggio pieces. The repetitive *i-m-i-m* is great for warming up, and playing the melody with *a* is ideal for adjusting your tone production.

CHECKLIST:

✔ Get a good, warm tone with the *a* finger.

✔ Your *a* free strokes should follow-through from the *knuckle joint* (the joint that connects the fingers to the hand). The amount of follow-through should be commensurate to the amount of pressure you apply to the string.

✔ If you have consistent tone problems, try a light rest stroke with *p*. This puts the *a* finger at a more advantageous angle resulting in a fatter tone.

✔ Plant *i* and *m* sequentially during the *i-m-i-m* exchanges.

✔ Prepare *p* and *a* on their respective strings at the same time. This happens right after *m* plays the last note of each measure.

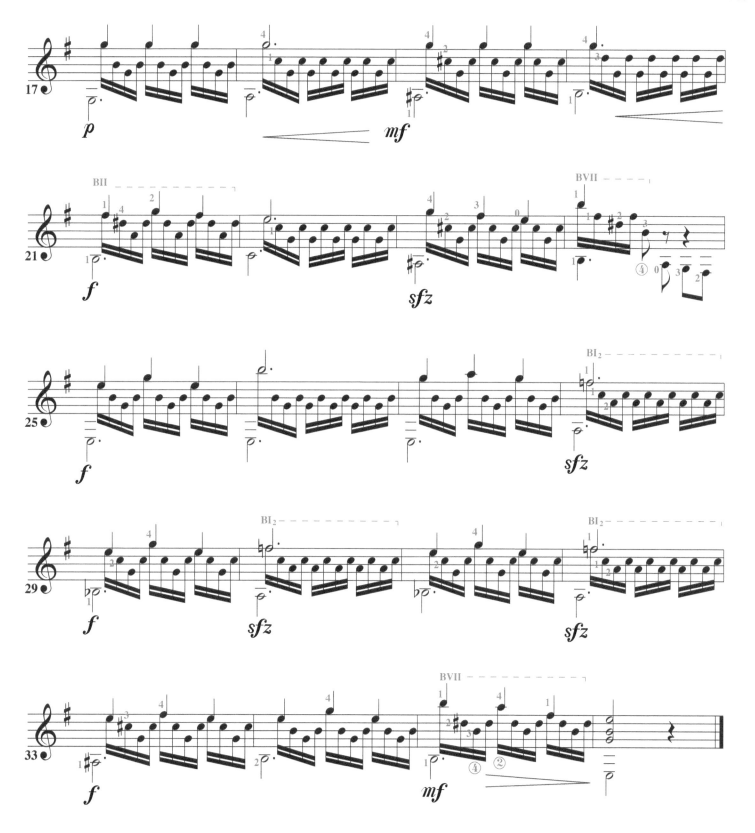

"J. S. Bach died from 1750 to the present."

• From a grade school essay on classical music. •

OPUS 35, #18

Fernando Sor   Track 18

CHECKLIST:

✔ Put *p* and *a* down on the strings at the same time, then…

✔ …put *i* and *m* down on their strings at the same time.

✔ Alternate planting in this way throughout the piece. Bring out the melody (stems up) with the *a* finger.

SORE STUDY

Fernando Sor/Scott Tennant

 Track 19

Sorry, Fernando! Can you ever forgive us? An irreverent re-working of Opus 31, Lesson 19 (Segovia's #10).

CHECKLIST:

✔ Play the repeated sixteenth notes with rest stroke, alternating *i* and *m*.

✔ The repeated sixteenth notes should be strong and even, but not heavy and labored. If your rest strokes have a quick release from the string, and spring back off the adjacent string, the notes will have a more desirable, light and bouncy sound.

✔ Phrase ("move" and crescendo) toward the downbeat of the bar, putting a slight accent on that note. This will make the sixteenths easier and lighter, and is a good tactic for making longer scale runs easier as well.

✔ Prepare the string-crossings carefully (as in the right-hand walking exercises).

✔ Observe the rests.

OPUS 60, #18

Fernando Sor Track 20

CHECKLIST:

✔ Note the chords that follow the arpeggios in measures 25 through 32. Even though the chords rapidly succeed the arpeggios, be sure *p*, *i* and *a* are prepared enough to produce a good tone on the chord.

✔ Also in measures 25 through 32 — keep the right hand still. Don't let it jump as you play the chords. Keep it stable; let the fingers do the work.

D.S. al Fine

OPUS 60, #24

Fernando Sor Track 21

CHECKLIST:

✔ Excellent speed burst work for arpeggios.

✔ Work towards evenness of the arpeggios.

Allegro Moderato
♩ = 100–132

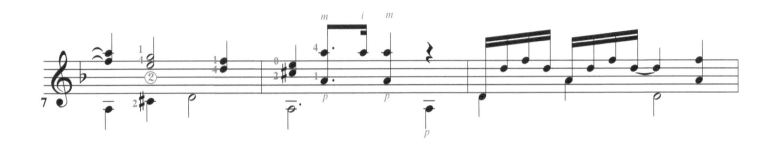

D.C. al Fine

"*Great things can be done by
great sacrifices only.*"

• Swami Vivekananda •

MALAGUEÑA

arr. Scott Tennant

Track 22

This exercise is preliminary preparation for Emilio Pujol's *El Abejorro* which is good fun; an arpeggio study imitating the flight of a big insect. HOWEVER, to insure you don't end up on the windshield, there are a few precautions to take. Study the "Checklist" carefully.

CHECKLIST:

✔ For maximum success at an eventual quick tempo, practice slowly at first, and sequentially plant each finger (i.e., plant *i* immediately after *p*, *a* immediately after *i*, *m* immediately after *a*, and *p* immediately after *m*, etc.).

✔ Practice both right-hand fingerings. Playing *p-i-m-i* is a great study, but for performance *p-i-a-m* is much more effective.

✔ Finish one group of notes before changing chords. Failure to do this results in a sloppy, choppy-sounding piece.

"I know what a sextet is, but I'd rather not say."

• From a grade school essay on classical music. •

ETUDE #13

Matteo Carcassi Track 23

Great beginning tremolo and arpeggio practice.

CHECKLIST:

✔ Begin the piece by preparing each triad with a full plant (planting *i* and *m* simultaneously). Prepare *p* after *i* plays the last repeated note.

✔ Progress to preparing each note of each arpeggio by planting the fingers sequentially, including *p*.

✔ Make sure the repeated notes played with an *a-m-i* exchange sound even in volume and tone. You may want to begin by practicing them *staccato* (short and disconnected) by exaggerating the planting and then progressing to *legato* (smooth and connected).

✔ Make sure both hands have completed each harmony before moving on. In other words, don't change chords with the left hand before the right hand has finished the figure.

✔ Play the indicated dynamics.

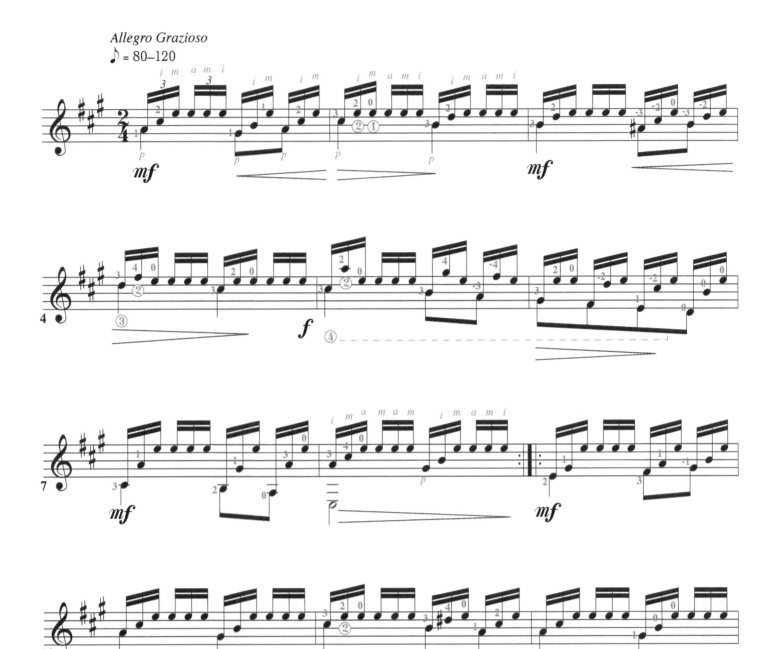

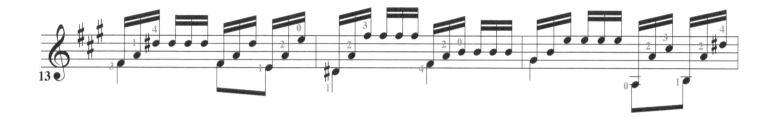

ETUDE #7

Matteo Carcassi Track 24

Good preliminary tremolo and arpeggio work.

CHECKLIST:

✔ Be sure the tremolo is even and pleasant-sounding. Don't be a speed demon.

✔ Be aware of and control the exchanges from *i* to *p* and from *p* to *a*.

✔ While learning the piece, it's good to use sequential planting in the right-hand fingers (prepare the fingers, one at a time, on the strings before playing). This includes *p*.

LITTLE LÄNDLER

Sköt Tennant **Track 25**

The best way to solidify your tremolo is to begin working out the problems by playing short bursts. Then, proceed to extended periods of tremolo. You may have already worked on the tremolo exercises in *Pumping Nylon*, including the single-string tremolo (very important). The goal of this next piece is to help you build confidence with short bursts of tremolo. Once this happens, you can string together these bursts into a more continuous, seamless tremolo while "feeling" shorter bursts with your right hand. This is the psychological aspect of tremolo, or any extended challenging technique. As our many individual breaths become breathing, so the "short bursts of tremolo" become just "tremolo." If you can perform two or three groups together successfully, you can just as easily do an entire piece.

CHECKLIST:

✔ If tremolo is a difficult issue with you, start by practicing each tremolo segment at the minimum metronome setting or slower. You don't necessarily have to play with the metronome, but at least use it to establish a tempo.

✔ As in the *Pumping Nylon* exercises, you'll play the notes of the tremolo detached. Also, keep them even in both volume and tone. Practicing slowly and staccato results in an even, articulate and controlled tremolo when played faster.

✔ Be SURE to plant *a* right after *p* plays, and to plant *p* right after *i* plays. Be especially aware of this during measures 17 through 24, where "long distance" string-skipping occurs.

✔ Play fairly staccato at a slow tempo, but *move* fast! Keep the fingers electrified; never lethargic. Release the strings as if they're hot; on fire. As you speed up the tempo, the speed of the movements will not change. The gaps between the notes will automatically get smaller. So, basically, you can increase the tempo without speeding up your movements!

✔ Make it your goal to progress toward playing the entire piece using continuous tremolo.

ETUDE #2

Matteo Carcassi Track 26

Good for tremolo and arpeggio improvement. Also great for working out the *m-a* exchange.

CHECKLIST:

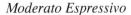

✔ Begin by preparing each chord with a full plant (*i*, *m* and *a* plant simultaneously), and playing the repeated notes staccato and evenly with an *m-a* exchange.

✔ Progress to planting the fingers sequentially and playing the repeated notes legato. You're simply training the fingers not to play the strings "from the air," (from far away with wider movements) and to control the tone and articulation by playing "from the strings," (close in to the strings with smaller movements).

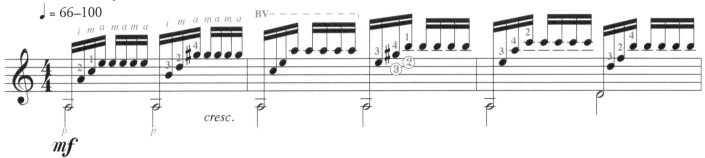

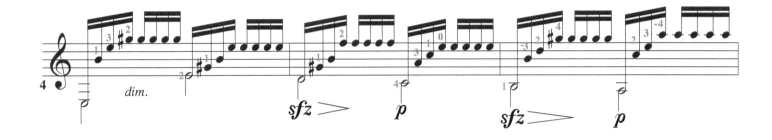

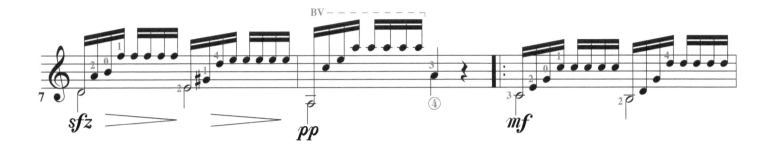

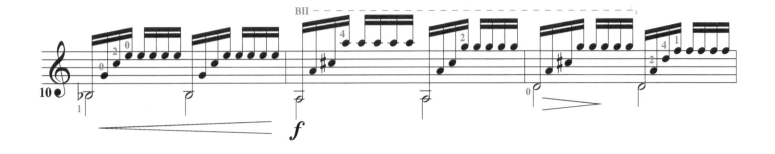

"People usually fail when they
are on the verge of success.
So give as much care to the end
as to the beginning;
then there will be no failure."

• Tao Te Ching •

TWO STUDIES

Francisco Tarrega

Estudio #12

Track 27

CHECKLIST:

✔ Listen for good tone. Producing a good tone while alternating *m* and *a* is often difficult due to extra rigidity (tension) that occurs in those fingers.

✔ Practice both rest stroke and free stroke.

✔ Produce equal tone and volume in all notes.

✔ Prepare (plant) especially well when skipping strings. For example, plant *i* on the downbeat of the second measure immediately after *a* has played the last note in the first measure, and plant *a* on the second sixteenth note of the second measure immediately after *i* has played. Continue in this way, much like the walking exercise.

✔ Synchronize right- and left-hand finger movements.

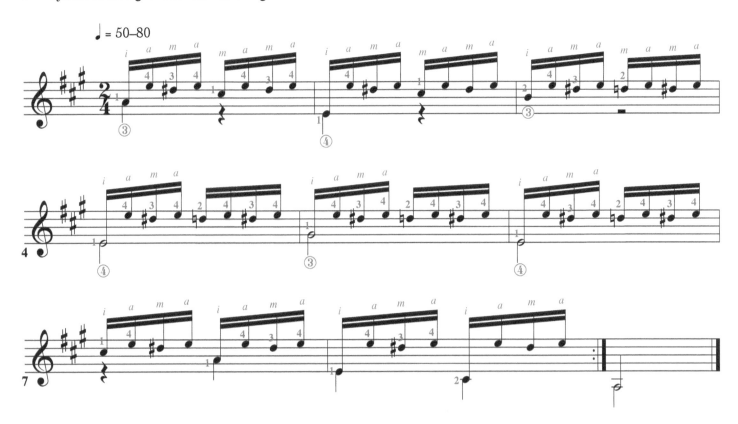

Estudio #3

Track 28

Great for *m-a* exchange study. This kind of work is beneficial for tremolo, as well.

CHECKLIST:

✔ Be sure *m* and *a* are even both in volume and tone.

✔ Be attentive to *i*'s tone when playing *p* and *i* together, especially on adjacent strings, as in the fifth measure.

ESTUDIO #3

ETUDE #6

Matteo Carcassi  Track 29

CHECKLIST:

✔ Play free stroke with *p*. Move it primarily from the *wrist joint* (where the thumb attaches to the wrist), and follow through toward the *i* and *m* fingers (as in making a fist), not directly downward. Work toward making the *p* melody legato and expressive. Strive for an even, round tone on both bass and treble strings.

Moderato
♩ = 80–108

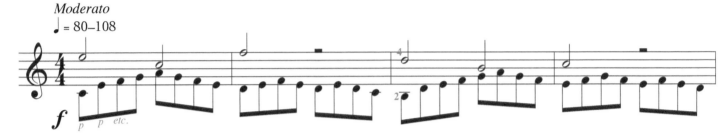

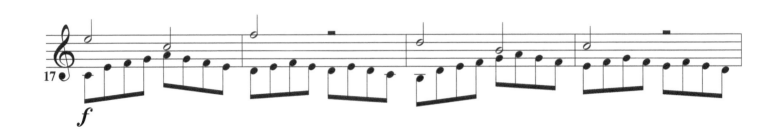

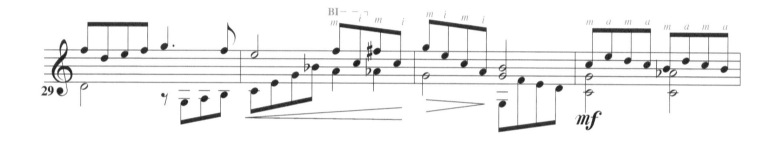

ETUDE #12

Matteo Carcassi   Track 30

CHECKLIST:

✔ Strive for a consistently even volume and tone with *p*. No one note played with *p* should stand out from the others.

✔ Be sure you completely finish the last note of each arpeggio with the right hand before moving on to the next harmony with the left.

✔ Observe the indicated dynamics.

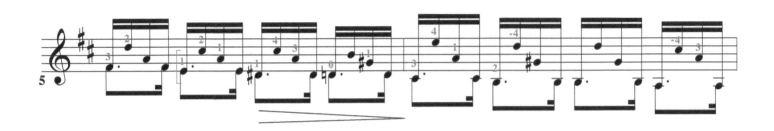

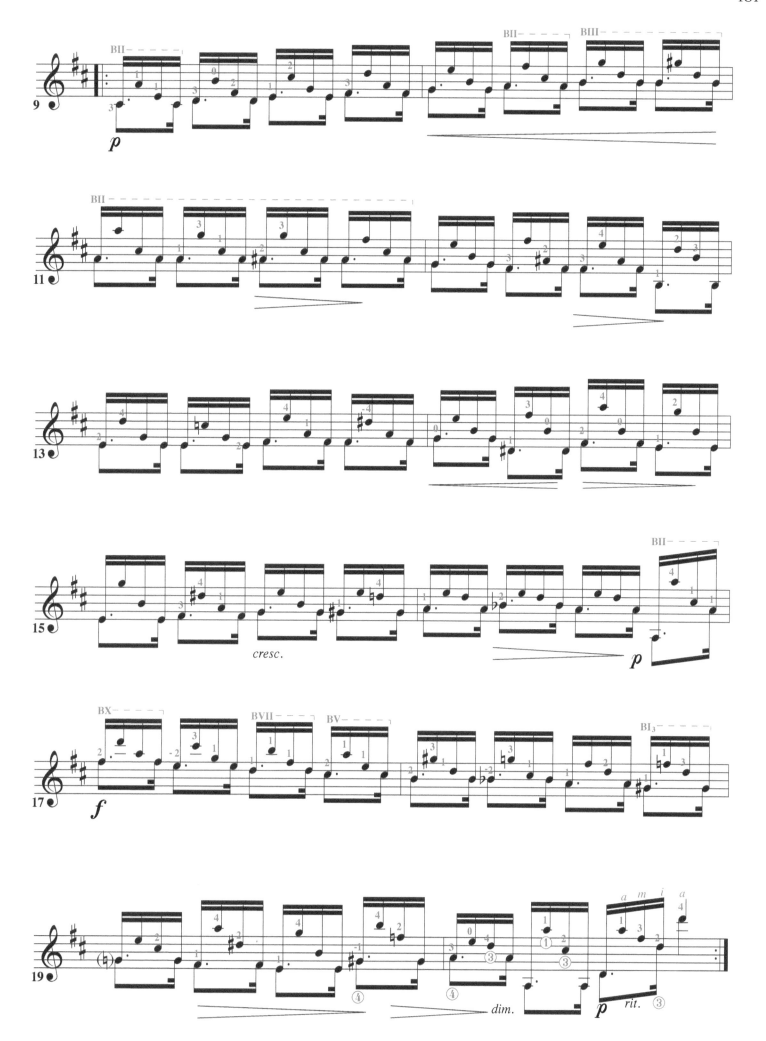

OPUS 6, STUDIO 4

Fernando Sor   Track 31

This is a good piece for practicing string-skipping and speed bursts. It is great for practicing the *p-i-p* exchange, too. Because of the cramped quarters between *p* and *i*, it can feel pinched and therefore produce a pinched, thin sound. Work on keeping the sound full. For the sake of further tone development, you should also try the two alternate fingerings.

CHECKLIST:

✔ After each chord, get the next right-hand finger down above the string it's going to play. Don't lounge around after the chord.

✔ Play the three notes of each burst evenly; avoid accenting with *p*.

OPUS 35, #19

Fernando Sor Track 32

CHECKLIST:

✔ Make sure the chords in the first eight bars are well-balanced. Feel your fingers digging into the strings. Sense the way the strings move under pressure from the fingertips.

✔ It is musically preferable to play *block chords* (with all of the notes sounded exactly together). Do not "roll" or arpeggiate them.

✔ As for the repeated-note triplets, practice them with all the indicated right-hand fingerings. Determine which

is best for you, or make up your own. Once you've decided, stick with that fingering.

✔ In measure 34 and similar bars, get the right-hand finger down to the 5th string for the "C" immediately after playing the preceding chord. When possible, plant the finger there; where there's a previous "C" ringing, keep the finger hovering over the string in preparation.

✔ Play the triplet figures slightly staccato for clarity and articulation.

STUDIO DE CAMPANELAS SU UN TEMA DELLA "FOLIA" DI M. DE FOSSA

(Study of Campenelas on a theme from "Folia" by M. de Fossa)

Francisco Tarrega

Track 33

Campanelas means "little bells." This refers to a ringing, arpeggio texture. The *folia* was a popular dance and chord progression known by all 16th, 17th and 18th century musicians—sort of like today's 12-bar blues. Obviously, some 19th century composers used it, too.

CHECKLIST:

✔ Plant the fingers sequentially, including *p*.

✔ Hold bass notes only for their written duration. Use either free left-hand fingers or *p* to stop open bass strings. The upper notes will be taken care of by the sequential planting.

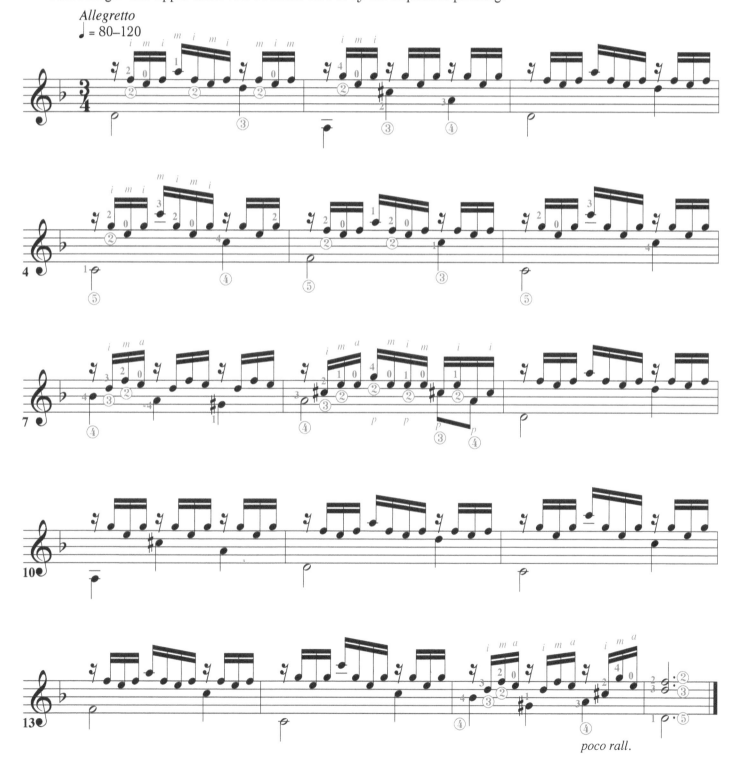

poco rall.

3 PAVANS

Luis Milan

A pavan is a type of dance. Milan felt that these should be played fairly quickly. These pavans are not only beautiful examples of Renaissance composition, but they offer an opportunity to improve one's chord balancing. As in *Balancing Act*, we will control this by adjusting the pressure of various right hand fingers.

✔ Balance all chords, slightly favoring the upper-most note in each chord (the melody), unless another line demands attention. For example, in *Pavan #1*, measure 5, the first C Major chord not only contains the "E" on the open 1st string, but requires the low "C" and the following four notes to be brought out with *p*.

✔ Hold all notes for their full durations. Pay special attention to the tied notes.

✔ Be sure the short scales in measures 18 and 19 of Pavan #1 are well synchronized, relaxed and smooth.

✔ For added improvement and some ear-training, and AFTER you've conquered the basics of the pieces, pick a line, starting with the melody, and sing it while playing the piece. Hold the notes where required. You'll hear the piece in an entirely different way. If your pet dog is lying on the floor listening to you practice, this should get him up and out-o'-there!

Pavan #1

Track 34

poco rit.

*hold 1 down

Pavan #2

Pavan #3

OPUS 44, #8

Fernando Sor

Track 37

CHECKLIST:

✔ Give each note its full value, but avoid excess ringing. For example, in measures 17 through 31, make sure the *Alberti bass** figures are clean by planting *i* and *p* sequentially, playing the top voice mainly with *m* and *a*.

* An Alberti bass is a repeated, broken-chord accompaniment pattern very common to early 19th century piano and guitar pieces.

OPUS 35, #5

Fernando Sor   Track 38

This study is good for shifts and improving your ability to think/visualize ahead.

CHECKLIST:

✔ Prepare the right-hand fingers appropriately (*p-i* or *p-m*), being careful to plant each quickly to avoid cutting off ringing notes. Don't play "from the air" but "from the string."

✔ Practice the left hand by preparing fingers for the next two sixteenths while playing the preceding two notes. Empty and lift off the fingers when they're finished. Think ahead.

✔ The shifts are small, so keep them quick and very easy.

*"Refrain means don't do it.
A refrain in music is the part
you better not try and sing."*

• From a grade school essay on classical music. •

SLUR STUDY

Mauro Giuliani Track 39

Slurs, slurs, and then some...

CHECKLIST:

✔ Don't lift left-hand fingers more than an inch above the strings.

✔ Make sure hammer-ons (ascending slurs) are quick and "snappy." Let the speed of the finger movement do the work, not muscle.

✔ When pulling-off (descending slurs), make a crisp sound by pulling-off down into the fingerboard, then emptying the finger.

✔ Feel each finger "fire" individually like a spark plug.

✔ Don't play the first note of a slur grouping too loudly. This will create an accent. We want everything to sound as even as possible.

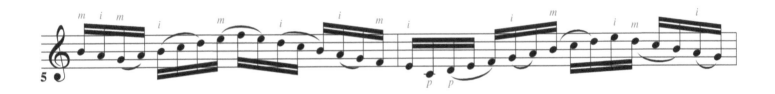

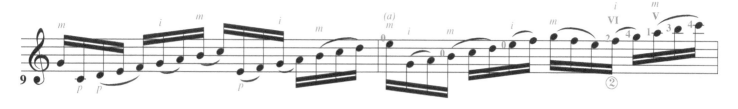

"What lies behind us
and what lies before us
are tiny matters compared to
what lies within us."

• Ralph Waldo Emerson •

OPUS 31, LEÇON XV

Fernando Sor Track 40

Now let's put those masterfully executed slurs to good use!

CHECKLIST:

✔ As in the previous Giuliani slur exercise, we're going to keep the fingers an inch or less above the string. No dive-bombing.

✔ Use speed instead of brawn in your slurs.

✔ Notice your left-hand tone during pull-offs. Sometimes calluses, a jagged nail edge or other things can produce a slightly scrapy sound as you pull across the string. You may need to experiment with the location on the fingertip, or keep any dry skin and calluses filed away or moisturized.

✔ Normally, we pull-off into the fingerboard for a crisp attack. HOWEVER, in a situation such as measures 17 through 19, where the pull-offs are on inner strings, we do not want to bump into the adjacent string and interrupt the upper note. In cases such as these, we have to execute our pull-off more like a "pull-up," missing the adjacent string during the release.

✔ Although the left-hand shifts are hardly difficult, don't make them so through tension. Make a conscious effort to keep the shifts light and easy. Often, the left hand tenses more during the notes directly following slurs—if the slurs are not tense, the following notes will not be tense.

OPUS 31, LEÇON XII

Fernando Sor Track 41

Don't let all that black ink frighten you. Overall, the tempo and feel of this piece are fairly leisurely.

CHECKLIST:

✔ Plant the quick notes of the arpeggios sequentially. Don't forget the thumb. Plant it right after *i* plays.

✔ Avoid the common tendency of playing the quick arpeggios and the slower notes that follow with two different dynamics. The quicker and slower notes should be of equal (or at least EXTREMELY SIMILAR) volume and fullness.

A PALE VIEW

David Pritchard Track 42

I'm happy to be able to include this piece. It is beautiful and fun to play. Although its nature is peaceful and slow, it is a culmination of many techniques presented in this book.

Pritchard's work employs steady underlying arpeggios throughout. Some of these require slurs to be accurately executed. The melody on top must be appropriately sustained, requiring great attention to right-hand tone as well as left-hand finger placement.

CHECKLIST:

✔ Arpeggios should be even, like flowing water.

✔ The melody must be round and voice-like.

✔ Be mindful of the hingebar (HB) in measure 17. Flatten the tip joint of your 1st finger to cover just the 5th, 4th and 3rd strings. The 2nd string must ring clearly.

✔ Keep the melody and arpeggios at two different dynamic levels, as if they were the right and left hands in a piano piece, or a singer and a guitarist.

✔ When you're familiar enough with the piece to play it from memory, close your eyes and go deeper into the finer points of playing, the most important being expression. Expression is communication. Talk through your guitar as you would recite a long-loved poem.

✔ Forget technique and enjoy...

202

D.S al Coda

*While holding the G♯ on the 6th fret of the 4th string with 4, lightly touch directly over the 18th fret with *i* and pluck the string with *a*.

AFTERWORD

This book has been an investment for you. It comes with a price tag, but your progress is free. It's true that we all have certain physical limits on the guitar, as we all have different physiques, joints, fingernails, skin, different finger-lengths, different guitar sizes, etc. Remember to keep the word "try" out of your vocabulary and simply do your best.

Think back to a time when you were a little kid. You were probably a great artist, right? The coloring book and construction paper were your canvases, waxy crayons were your paints and the refrigerator door was your personal art gallery. The praise was thick, and there were no critics. The semi-stick figures were vividly real to you. You saw no boundaries, no limits to your talent. What happened to that?

When you ask a class of kindergarteners, first or second graders, "Who here plays guitar?" you'll get a roomful of hands in the air. "Sure I can play guitar! Why not? What's a guitar?" We need to retrieve that attitude and enthusiasm that we put aside as we did our toys. In that frame of mind, there really are no boundaries and the possibilities are endless.

So do your best. Put aside physical limitations, and keep in mind that it's music we want to make. And remember what those kindergarteners already know: MUSIC IS FUN. Do the work so you can enjoy yourself afterwards. Good luck!

> *"The thing we fear the most is not that we will shrivel up and become insignificant little people.*
> *The thing we fear the most is that we could become as big and grand as we are capable of becoming."*

• Nelson Mandela •

SECOND EDITION

COMPLETE PUMPING NYLON

PART 3

Intermediate to
Advanced Repertoire

Audio tracks recorded at Take One Studios, Freiburg, Germany, and
Penguin Studios, Pasadena, CA; mastered at Bar None Studio, Northford, CT

CONTENTS

This table of contents is designed to help you use this section as effectively as possible. Not only will it give you an "at-a-glance" tour of what the section contains and help you find the specific piece you seek, but it will also help you find pieces that relate to the specific areas of technique you wish to study. For the most part, pieces appear in rough chronological order, with exceptions here and there to avoid unnecessary page turns during pieces. The categories of technique are shown across the top. The box(es) checked next to a piece tell you which technique(s) apply to that piece. The technique categories are taken directly from the first section of this book. We hope you enjoy it. —*Nathaniel Gunod*

PREFACE

Welcome! The pieces in this section are more advanced than the repertoire in the previous section. They are primarily concert pieces instead of the shorter, more pedagogical etudes presented in the *Easy to Early Intermediate* section. Therefore, the pieces tend to be longer and much more substantial. Consider this book to be a brief representation of the types of pieces that contain specific technique-building elements (such as concentrated scales, left-hand slurs, arpeggios, tremolo and the like). When practiced correctly and with the proper intent, they will aid in developing your guitar-playing skills.

In our continuing quest to serve you something new and tasty to consume, we have made an effort to put some newer pieces on your plate. We hope to not only help you enjoy significant progress, but to also open your eyes and ears to new, delightful concert pieces to perform for the enjoyment of others.

A "checklist" of specific issues upon which to focus—such as technical and/or musical challenges, fingering and practicing tips—precedes each piece. If taken to heart, these pieces should be of great benefit to you.

As always, it is a good idea to check your progress with a teacher when problems arise, as there is no ideal substitute for expert advice. I encourage you to take the ideas presented in each piece and expand on them yourself. Find other pieces that will further help you overcome any obstacles. You have what it takes to play anything, and with some mindful practice, you will!

Glossary of Signs and Terms

This list will help you to interpret the various markings in the music.

1, 2, 3, 4......................Left hand fingers, numbered from index (1) to pinky (4).

p, i, m, a......................Right hand fingers: *p* = thumb, *i* = index, *m* = middle, *a* = ring finger.

①②③④⑤⑥..............The six strings of the guitar, numbered from low E⑥ to high E①.

IV, V, VII, etc. ....Roman numerals. Used to indicate frets. Here is a quick review of these symbols: I=1, II=2, III=3, IV=4, V=5, VI=6, VII=7, VIII=8, IX=9, X=10, XI=11 and XII=12.

BII₄.............................The B indicates a barre. The Roman numeral indicates the fret to be barred, and the small number indicates the amount of strings to be barred. So, this symbol indicates to barre four strings at the second fret.

-1, -2, -3, -4 ....A dash in front of a fingering indicates a *guide finger shift*. A *shift* is a movement from one position to another. A *guide finger* is a finger that can be used just before and just after a shift. For instance, if the 4th finger has been used to play G on the 1st string, 3rd fret, and then moves to play A on the 1st string, 5th fret, it will be marked -4 .

⑥ = D...........................Tune the 6th string down to D.

⊕ ....*Coda* sign. Marks the ending section of a piece.

𝄋 ....*Segno*. When playing a D. S. al Fine form, go back to this sign and play to the end.

♩ = 60 ....Tempo marking. In this case, the metronome should be set to 60. Each click represents a quarter note.

♩ ⨪ ....*Accent*. Emphasize.

♩ · ....*Staccato*. Short. Detached.

♩ ‾ ....*Tenuto*. To hold a note for its full value.

a tempo ....Return to the original *tempo* or speed.

Allegro...............................Lively, cheerful, fast.

Andante..............................A moderate, walking tempo.

Andantino ....Slightly faster than *andante*.

cresc.................................*Crescendo*. Gradually becoming louder.

decresc...............................*Decrescendo*. Gradually becoming softer.

dim..................................*Diminuendo*. Gradually becoming softer.

D. C. al *Coda* ....Go back to the beginning of the piece and play to the coda indication, then skip down to the *Coda*.

D. C. al *Fine*.....................Da Capo al Fine. Go to the beginning and play until the *Fine*.

D. S. al *Fine* ....Dal Segno al Fine. Go back to the sign 𝄋 and play until the *Fine*.

Fine ....The end.

Moderato............................In a moderate tempo.

molto ....Very.

morendo ....Dying away.

mosso ....Moved. Agitated.

poco ritenuto ....Immediately becoming a little held back or slower.

rall. ....*Rallentando*. Becoming gradually slower.

rit....................................*Ritardando*. Becoming gradually slower.

simile...............................When this word appears after a pattern has been established (fingerings, dynamics, etc.), it means to continue in this manner.

sub..................................*Subito*. Suddenly.

Tranquillo.......................Tranquil, calm, quiet.

DYNAMIC SIGNS

p ....*Piano*. Soft.

pp ....*Pianissimo*. Very soft.

mp ....*Mezzo piano*. Moderately soft.

f ....*Forte*. Loud.

ff ....*Fortissimo*. Very loud.

mf ....*Mezzo forte*. Moderately loud.

fp ....*Forte piano*. Strike a loud note and suddenly become soft.

sfz ....*Sforzando*. A sudden strong accent.

◁ ....*Crescendo*. Gradually becoming louder

▷ ....*Decrescendo*. Gradually becoming softer.

THE FROG GALLIARD

John Dowland/
arr. S. Tennant Track 43

I include this piece mainly because it is one of my favorite works by perhaps my favorite composer. I never tire of playing it, and I hope you will derive as much joy from it as I have over the years. Also, it offers some good opportunities for us to work out those nasty *a-i* scale passages we usually avoid! Note that the 3rd string is tuned to F♯.

CHECKLIST:

✔ Keep the overall feel of the piece light. Use primarily free-stroke throughout.

✔ For the scale passages, I suggest using free stroke *a-i* alternation, as these fingers are further away from each other than are *i-m*, creating a better balance in the hand and thus allowing for greater evenness and fluidity in the lines. This exchange may feel awkward at first, but will soon become your favored fingering pattern for many quick, light passages.

FANTASIA #18

Luis Milan/
transcribed by S. Tennant   Track 44

This Fantasia comes from Milan's book, *El Maestro*, published in Spain in 1536. We've come to interpret the word "maestro" as a "master" of one's instrument or profession but it also means "teacher." This collection of pieces leans heavily toward the pedagogical side, as these fantasias contain many elements that a student needs to deal with while learning the fingerboard and technique. This piece is particularly good for scale and string-crossing practice.

CHECKLIST:

✔ Don't forget to tune your third string to F♯.

✔ Balance chords well, pressing slightly harder with the appropriate right-hand finger to bring out the melody.

✔ Prepare a finger well when it has to skip over one or more strings.

✔ Scales may be played with the right-hand fingering indicated or with *i-a*, *p-i* or *p-m*.

✔ A capo may be used at the 2nd or 3rd fret for a more "authentic" simulation of the vihuela's pitch. The vihuela was the Renaissance instrument closest to the modern guitar. Milan's instructions were to tune the top string "as high as it will go." It is also helpful for the left hand as the frets are a little closer together in the 3rd position than in the open position.

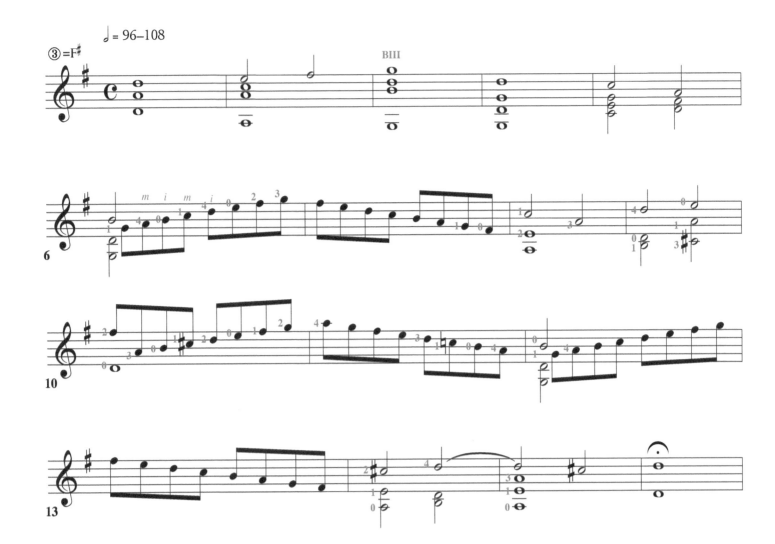

214

When we dwell on our past mistakes and fears,
we relive them daily.
Review and learn from them, and then
THROW THEM AWAY.
They're a waste of time otherwise.

FANTASIA #16

Luis Milan/
transcribed by S. Tennant   Track 45

Also from *El Maestro*, this is a shorter fantasia covering the same technical points as *Fantasia #18* (page 212).
I have transcribed it with the 3rd string tuned to "G," as opposed to the "F#" tuning, because of the key and
for general convenience of fingering—the "F#" tuning creates some fairly awkward fingerings in this piece.
Review the checklist on page 212 before continuing.

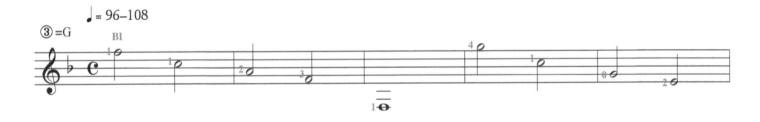

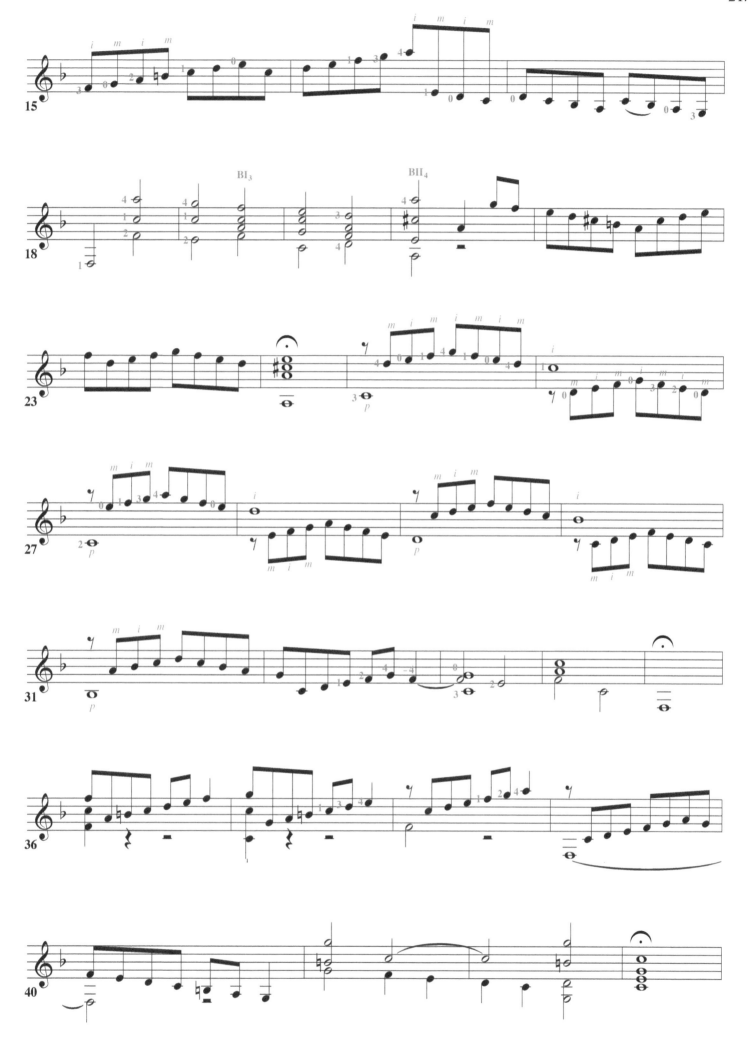

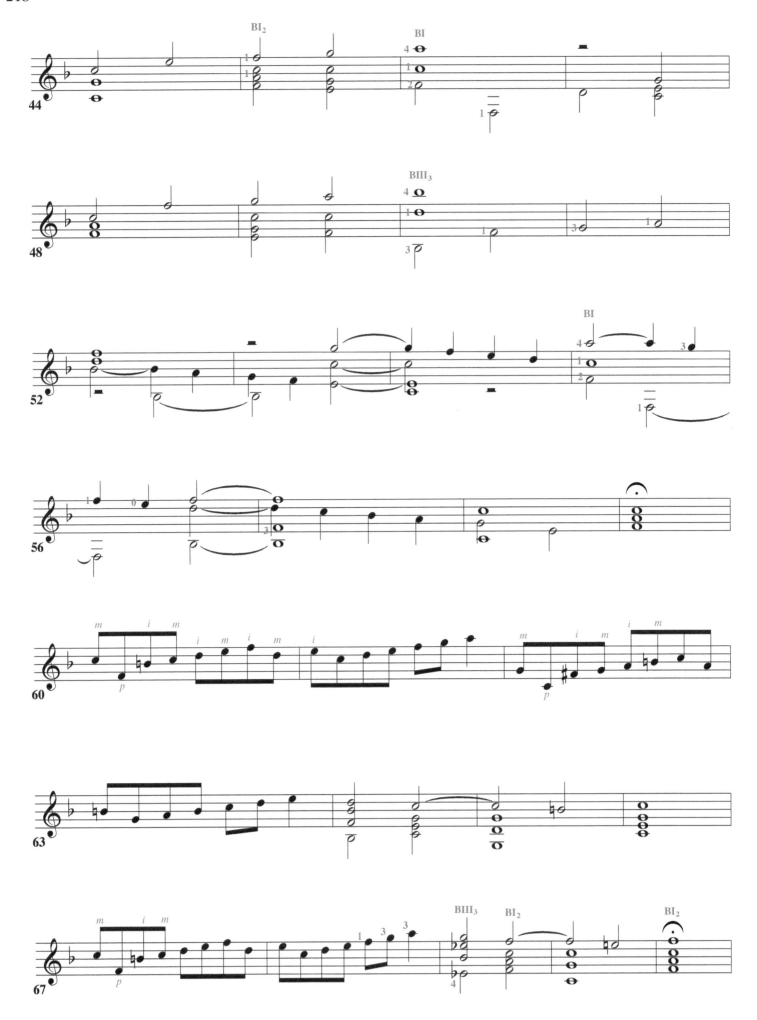

VEINTIDÓS DIFERENCIAS DE CONDE CLAROS

Luis de Narváez/
transcribed by S. Tennant

Track 46

This is one of my favorite all-time pieces and my favorite setting of *Conde Claros*, a famous Spanish chord sequence. It is an excellent piece for scale work.

CHECKLIST:

✔ Aim for well-balanced, chorale-like chords.

✔ Aim for smooth scales.

✔ Shape the lines. A good way to start is to go up (louder) when the line goes up, and down (softer) when the line comes down. This is general advice and as the piece becomes more familiar, your own phrasing and idea shaping will surface.

* Editorial. Tempo indication not in the original edition.

Ritardando

You were born with all the abilities you will ever want.
Your efforts are meant simply to remove the obstacles that keep you from seeing them.

VARIATIONS SUR LES "FOLIES D'ESPAGNE," OP. 45

Mauro Giuliani

Track 47

A typical and lovely variation set, loaded with all your favorite technical treats.

CHECKLIST:

✔ In general, the classic performance practice for a theme and variations set is to play the variations in more or less the same tempo as the theme, until indicated. However, I like to vary each one in tempo slightly to further "vary" each variation.

✔ In Variation I, prepare the fingers very carefully when skipping strings. Although there's some room for expression, the eighth notes should remain fairly smooth and constant.

✔ In Variation II, make the slurs clean and articulate. To achieve this, keep the left-hand fingers as close to their strings as possible, releasing the force from each finger after each slur.

✔ In Variation III, I think the most important thing is to make the chord changes clean by shifting *only* when the last note of the previous chord has sounded for its *full* value.

✔ Variation IV is best prepared slowly while placing the left-hand fingers above their notes one note in advance (when possible). For instance, in measure one, beat one, the 2nd finger will hover right over the A (3rd string) while the octave Ds are being played, and so on. Shape it well and try to avoid the ringing of any stray notes.

✔ In Variation V, avoid the unflattering tendency to let notes ring when the melody shifts to the thumb in measure 9. Control the thumb's tone by playing the string from a close distance.

✔ Help make Variation VI articulate by observing the rests.

228

Var. III

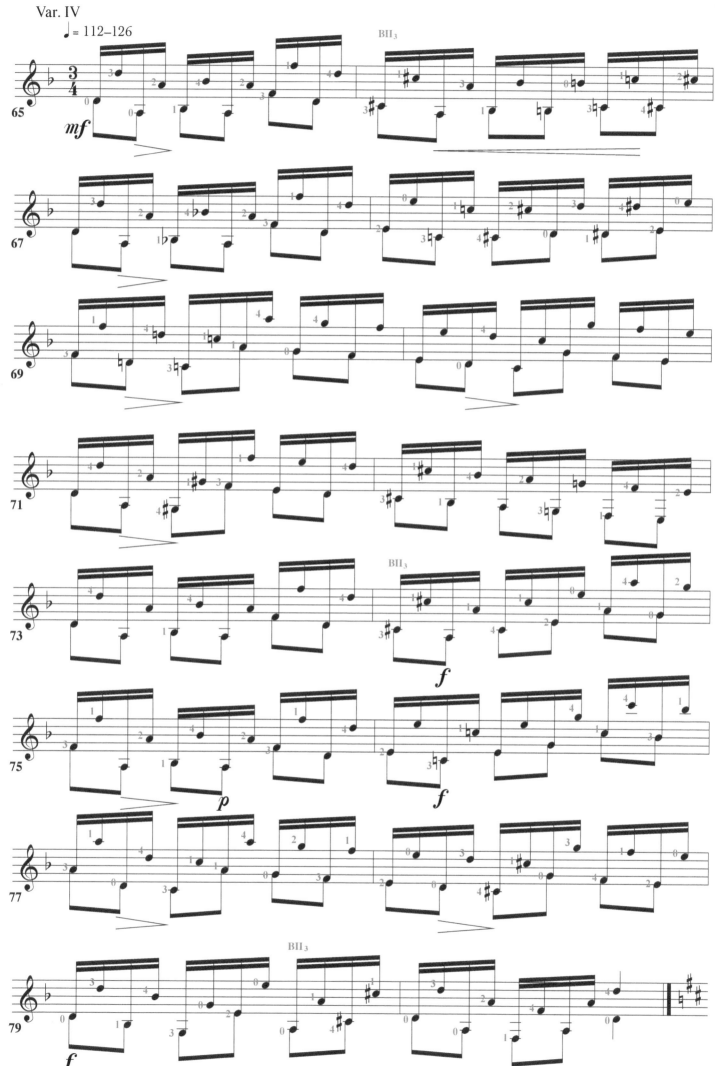

Var. V *Un poco piu adagio*

♩ = 84–96

Var.VI

Allegro Vivace

♩ = 152–176

235

ETUDE #11

Napoléon Coste

Track 48

This study comes from a popular collection of 25 etudes for guitar, Op. 38. Coste played a seven-string guitar so many of the bass notes have been altered slightly. This piece is great for practicing slurs and shifts.

CHECKLIST:

✔ Although we're focusing on slurs and shifting here, do not neglect the chords. Make them sound well balanced with a good, round tone.

✔ Observing the rest after each chord as indicated will allow you extra time to get to the slurs. Use this as transit time to "spot," or look at and get to, the appropriate frets for the slurs.

✔ You may notice (depending on your guitar) that you need to exert a bit more force, or "snap," to execute the slurs on the bass strings than you do on the trebles.

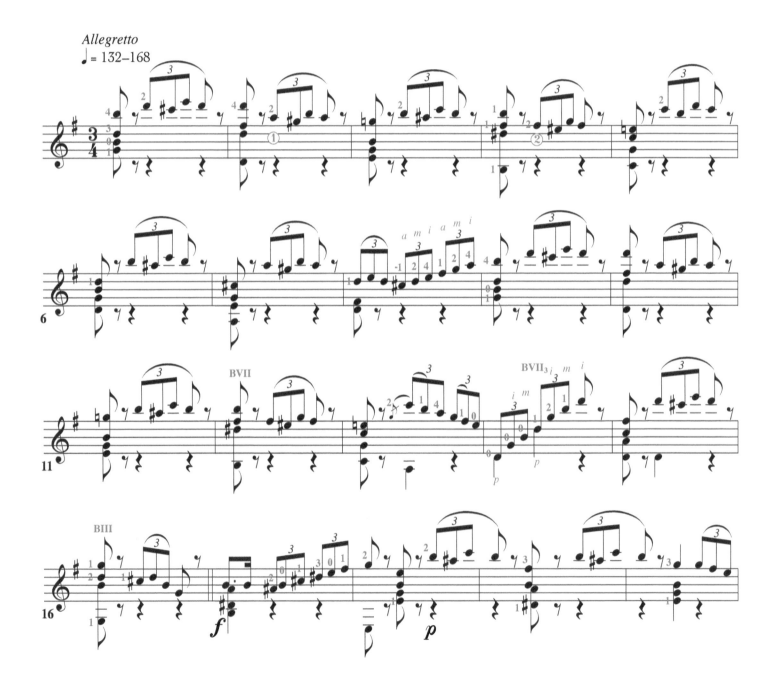

FANTASIA ORIGINAL
CAPRICHO Á IMITACIÓN DEL PIANO

José Viñas

Track 49

This piece by Viñas carries the subtitle: *"Capricho a imitación del Piano,"* or "Capricho (or *capriccio*—an instrumental piece in a free form) in imitation of a Piano." This style becomes apparent with the repeated, piano-like chords in measures 9 and 10, and the chordal theme starting in measure 15.

CHECKLIST:

✔ Balance all chords well, making each voice clear—as they would sound on a piano.

✔ Make the chords in measures 9 and 10 as smooth and connected as possible.

✔ Keep the overall feeling of the *Introduction (Andante Mosso)* legato.

✔ In contrast, make sure the accents, such as those in measures 14–17 and 23–25, are taken into account. Also, pay attention to the rests in measures 22–30.

✔ At first, I suggest learning the tremolo section without the tremolo. First, practice the chords in rhythm—without tremolo—to master the chord changes and shifts. Then add the tremolo. Much of the trouble in tremolo pieces comes from awkward left-hand movements, thereby throwing the right hand out of synchronization with the left.

✔ The tremolo can be added all at once (if you are confident of your tremolo) or gradually, adding one note, then two and finally three.

✔ The same strategy can be applied to the arpeggio section beginning in measure 65.

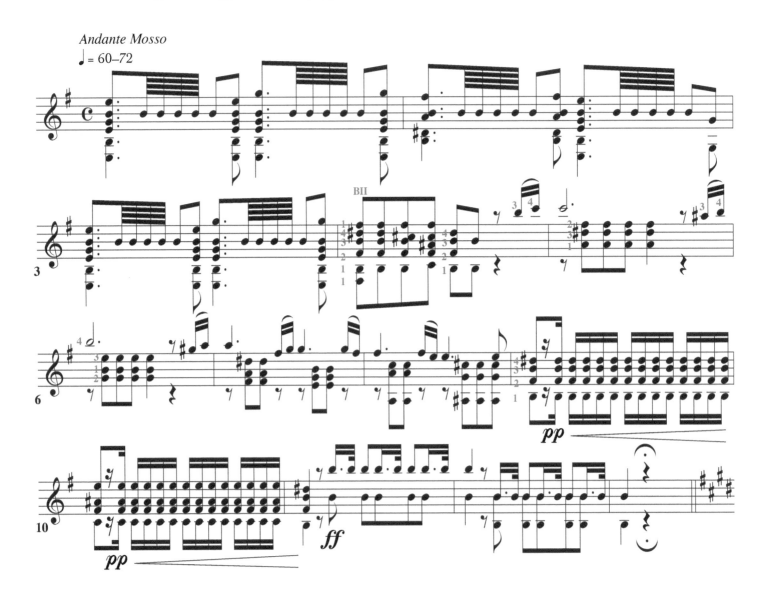

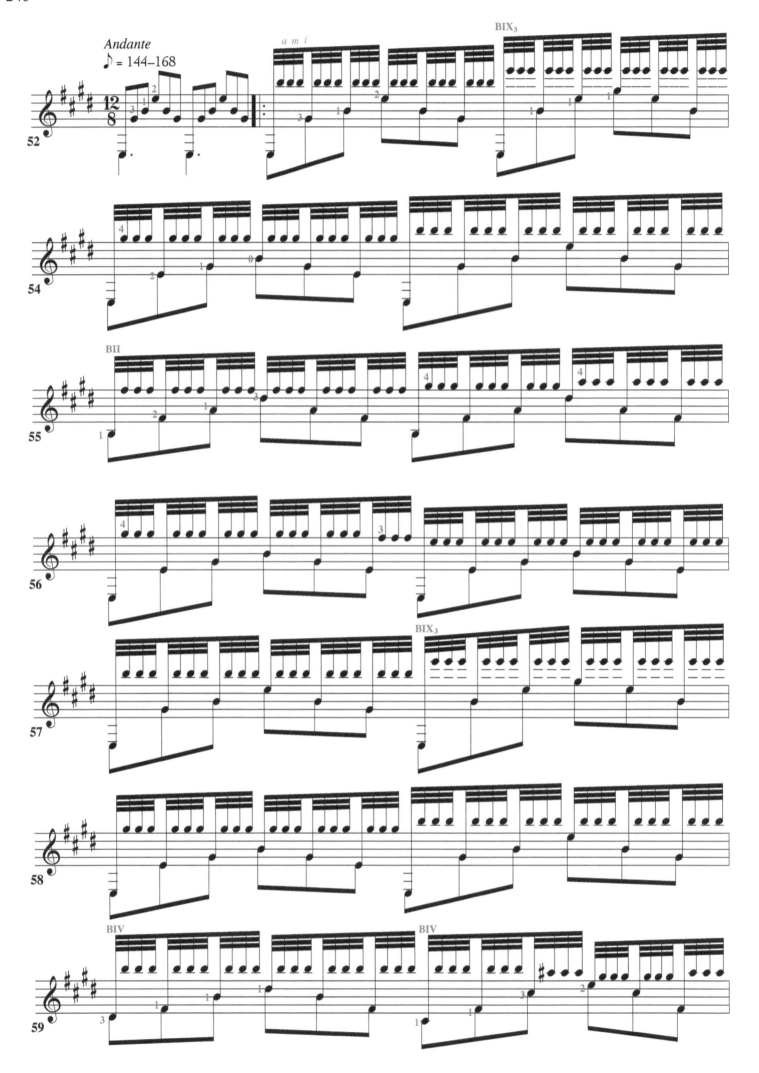

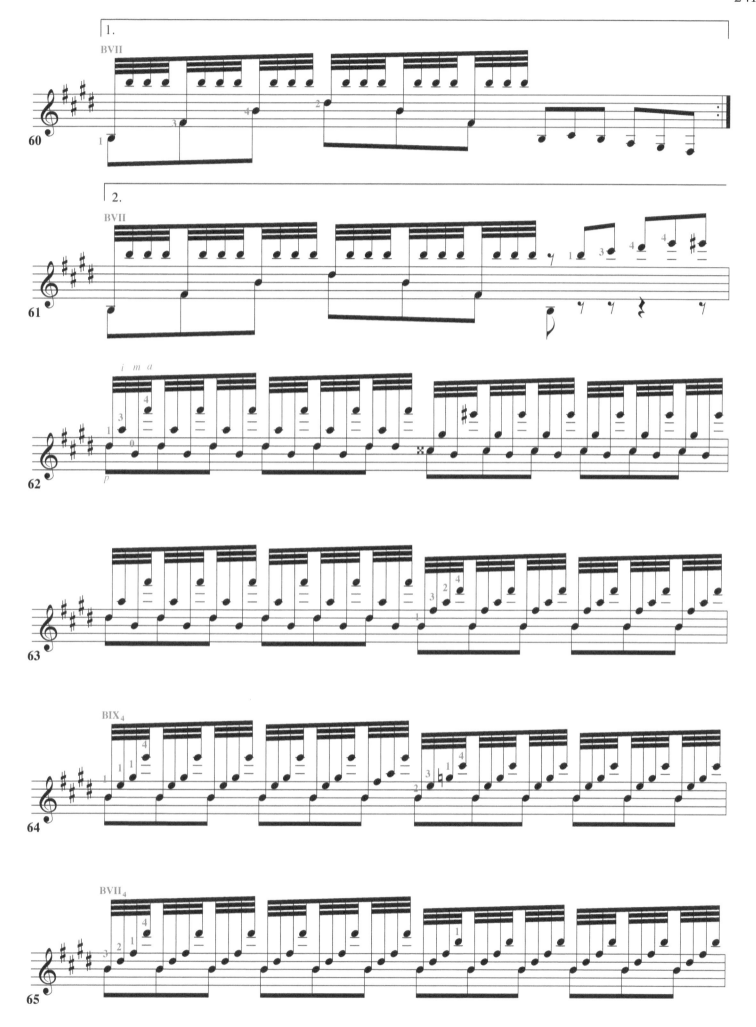

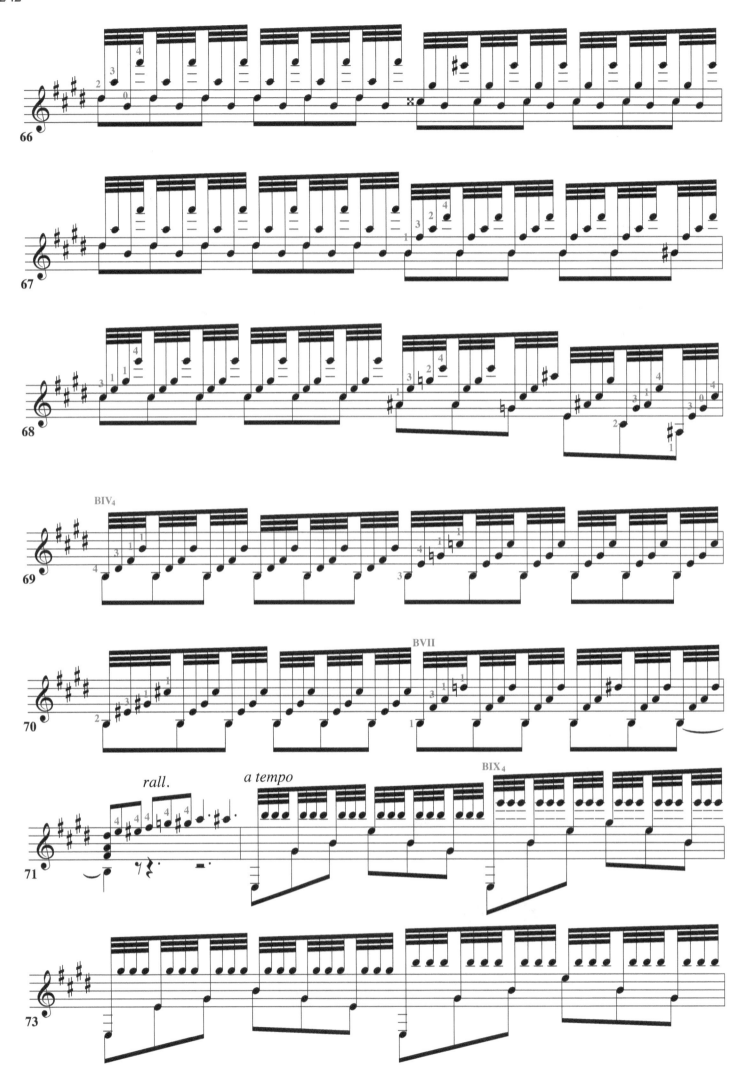

244

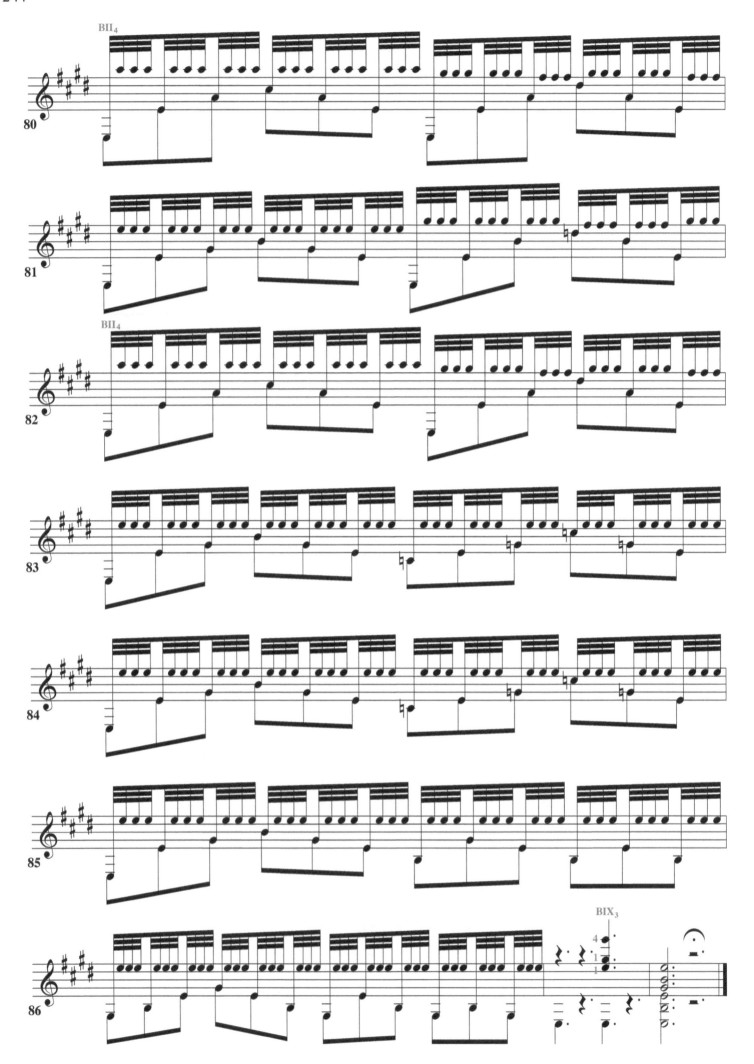

RASGUEADO EXERCISE IN SOLEÁ
Adam del Monte

Track 50

Adam del Monte is a phenomenal flamenco and classical guitarist. He received his classical training at the Royal Northern College of Music in Manchester, England, and soon after went on to master the flamenco guitar during his many years in Spain, where he studied with the likes of Pepe "Habichuela" and Gerardo Nuñez. He was the first-prize winner of the 1997 Stotsenberg Competition, and has since been touring the globe as a highly sought-after flamenco artist. Adam can be heard performing his pieces on the recording for this book. The *Soleá* is played in a twelve-beat pattern. Accents in this pattern occur on beats 3, 6, 8, 10 and 12. Technically, this study and the one to follow (page 248) are difficult but if broken down into segments, can be dealt with much more effectively.

CHECKLIST:

✔ I suggest you practice your rasgueado patterns separately first. This way you may avoid mental blocks and hang-ups later in the piece.

✔ This "exercise" offers much more than rasgueados. A typical flamenco pattern of an arpeggio followed immediately by a quick scale run can be found in measures 17–23, and should be practiced separately. To aid in the ease of the scales, always play through to the downbeat of the next bar, which is played with p. This will help you psychologically and make the scales more legato.

✔ Observe the note changes within the rasgueado patterns beginning in measure 25.

✔ The *golpe*, or "tap" in bar 38 would traditionally be done on the tap plate on the top of the guitar with the right-hand *a* or *c* fingernail. If you don't have a tap plate or a flamenco guitar and don't want to hurt your finish, you can either tape an old credit card or similar piece of thick plastic to the top of your guitar, or simply be careful and tap with the fleshy part of your *a* fingertip.

* Variations:

Opt: "*p*" may rest on ⑥ here

tap

*simultaneous rasqueado with i and p

© Adam del Monte, 1999. Used by Permission.

ALZAPUA AND THUMB STUDY IN SOLEÁ *Adam del Monte*

Track 51

Alzapua is a flamenco technique where the thumb plays up and down over one or several strings. As I mentioned in the first section of this book, this is a fantastic exercise for developing the right-hand thumb, and developing the thumb is something we, as classical guitarists, routinely neglect.

CHECKLIST:

✔ Again, go back and review this alzapua technique on page 72. It's always a good idea to approach a piece with a running start.

✔ Play primarily rest strokes with the thumb. This may require that you move your right hand down toward the floor a bit to get your thumb in an advantageous position. The rest strokes don't have to be heavy. Keep them light (but very audible!).

✔ Wherever the thumb plays quick, consecutive notes on adjacent strings, such as in measures 17–23, make it easier on yourself by dragging the thumb across the strings in a controlled manner, thus letting gravity do much of the work.

✔ The actual alzapua pattern, which first occurs in measure 9, must be executed by rest-stroking the first sixteenth note of the pattern, thus automatically setting up the thumb for the up- and down-strokes on the chords that immediately follow.

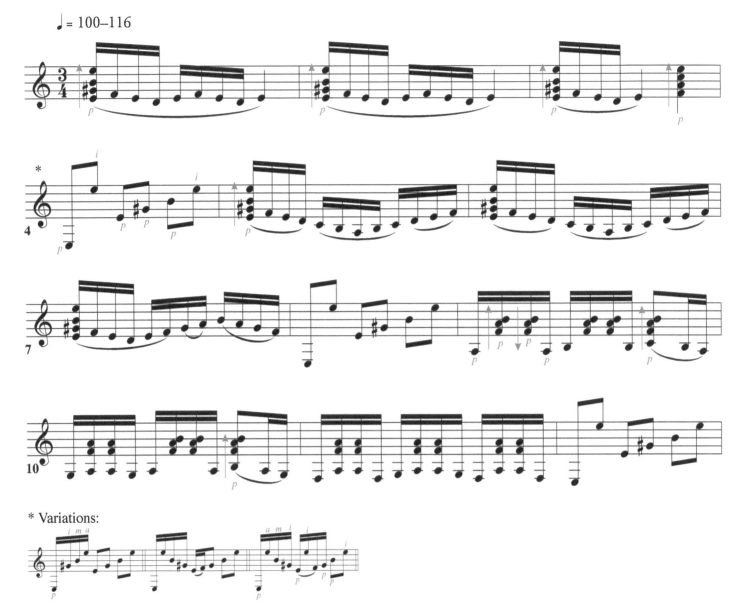

* Variations:

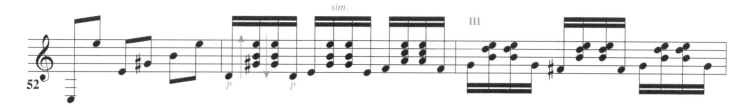

On nervousness and loving what you do:

"Love overcomes fear.
Fear cannot exist in the presence
of love."

• Pepe Romero •

INSPIRED BY VILLA-LOBOS ETUDE #1

Joe Diorio

Track 52

Joe Diorio is one of the most innovative jazz greats playing the guitar today. When I found out that he had reharmonized some traditional classical guitar etudes, I immediately asked him for his permission to include this one. Perhaps you will find a fresh enthusiasm for the piece, as I did. It presents some new challenges not found in its traditional counterpart.

CHECKLIST:

✔ Learn the right-hand pattern separately on open strings or just a single chord.

✔ The right-hand pattern will come easier and quicker if you apply sequential *planting*. To plant, prepare the fingers on the strings just before playing. In sequential planting, the individual fingers are prepared on their strings—one at a time—just before striking.

✔ Learn the chords separately. In a way, the chords pose more of a technical challenge than the right-hand pattern does. At least the right-hand pattern remains fairly constant once you learn it.

✔ Note the awkward barre in measure 12! Don't hurt yourself. Practice it slowly at first.

✔ The composer offers an optional ending, so suit yourself.

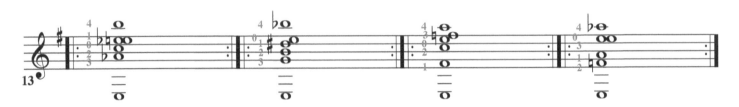

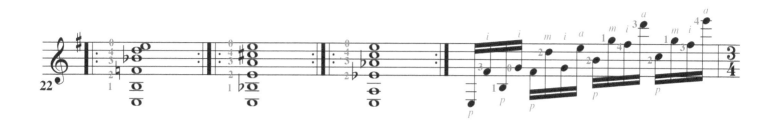

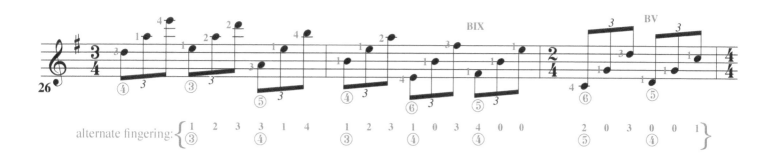

alternate fingering:

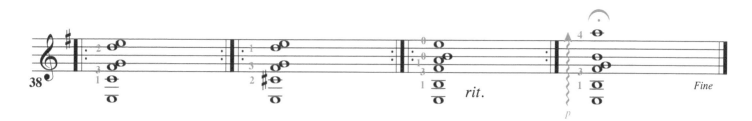

Optional ending (substitute this line for measures 36 through 41)

STUDY #1

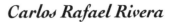

Carlos Rafael Rivera   Track 53

Carlos Rivera is a talented composer of Cuban heritage living in Southern California. His composition *Whirler of the Dance* was the set piece for the 1998 GFA competition. His music has passion and drive and is heavily Latin-based.

CHECKLIST:

✔ Despite the accents and quick tempo, the piece should maintain a fluidity throughout. Note the composer's indication, "Flowing."

✔ The accents may be done with either rest stroke or free stroke, depending on the depth-of-sound desired. Keep in mind, though, the dynamic indications.

✔ There are several places, such as the first note in measure 5, that have an accent over a slurred note. Instead of slamming the finger harder into the fretboard, play the first note of the slur softer, fighting the tendency to accent the first note of a slur.

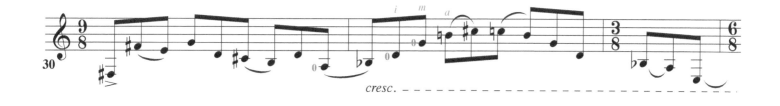

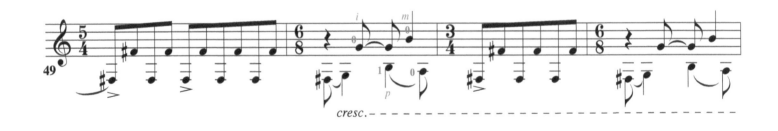

"Have you ever seen a cloud make an aesthetic mistake?"

• Alan Watts •

PLAINTE

Brian Head

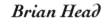
Track 54

Those familiar with *Pumping Nylon* are familiar with Brian Head and his two pieces in that book, *Chant* and *Fanfare*. *Plainte* is a movement from Head's suite, which opens with *Fanfare*. In *Plainte*, the challenges are aimed at both the left *and* right hands.

CHECKLIST:

✔ Make sure all notes are held for their appropriate value.

✔ The right hand's job is to bring out the appropriate voices when marked. This can be a bit challenging at first because of the *stretto* (overlapping counterpoint, where voices enter quickly behind one another).

✔ The first note of the two-note motive should be slightly stressed.

262

Practice does not make perfect.
PERFECT practice makes perfect.

CONCIERTO DE ARANJUEZ
CADENZA (FROM ADAGIO: 2ND MOVEMENT)

Joaquín Rodrigo

Track 55

This piece is a favorite of many and this is the passage that made me want to play the classical guitar when I was a boy. Here are some things to do:

CHECKLIST:

✔ As with all music, the most important thing to remember here is to be expressive. Although the technical preparation is important for achieving a level of comfort and confidence, don't let yourself get bogged down with the technical side only. This can be an addictive slump for some folks.

✔ While it may be unconventional, I feel most comfortable fingering the right hand as marked in measures 1–4 for musical reasons. If I were to play the repeated G♯s on the 6th string with p, which is the most tempting thing to do, I wouldn't be able to speed up and slow down as much as I would like. Also, the thumb tends to naturally produce a heavier tone and I want to avoid this; I want the emphasis to be on the upper part of the line, which is the melody. So, begin preparing for the string skipping by choosing a comfortably slow tempo and practice this passage in strict rhythm, with no rubato.

✔ Keep the slurs strong!

✔ In measures 6 and 7, practice the notes played with p staccato. This is to train the thumb to stay very, very close to the string. When taken at tempo, the staccato can be either softened or omitted, but the thumb should remain in control.

✔ The "sweeps" in measures 10, 12 and 21–24 are the most challenging passages in this cadenza. To be able to play these well and with control, you shouldn't just run the finger randomly back and forth over the strings. Note that the right-hand fingering offered here is half arpeggio, half sweep. Therefore, practice them as arpeggios, making sure to play each note with control and clarity. This, as usual, requires some slow work at the beginning. Don't worry about having to play these very fast. Take your time with them in performance and make them harp-like and beautiful.

✔ From measure 25 to the end, we "rock out." I offer a couple of alternate right-hand fingerings here. The first is unconventional but works well and feels comfortable after you get used to it. The second one is more reasonable, perhaps, and might serve you better. Regardless of the fingering you eventually come up with, it must be strong and fast! This is the climax to beat all climaxes!

CADENZA

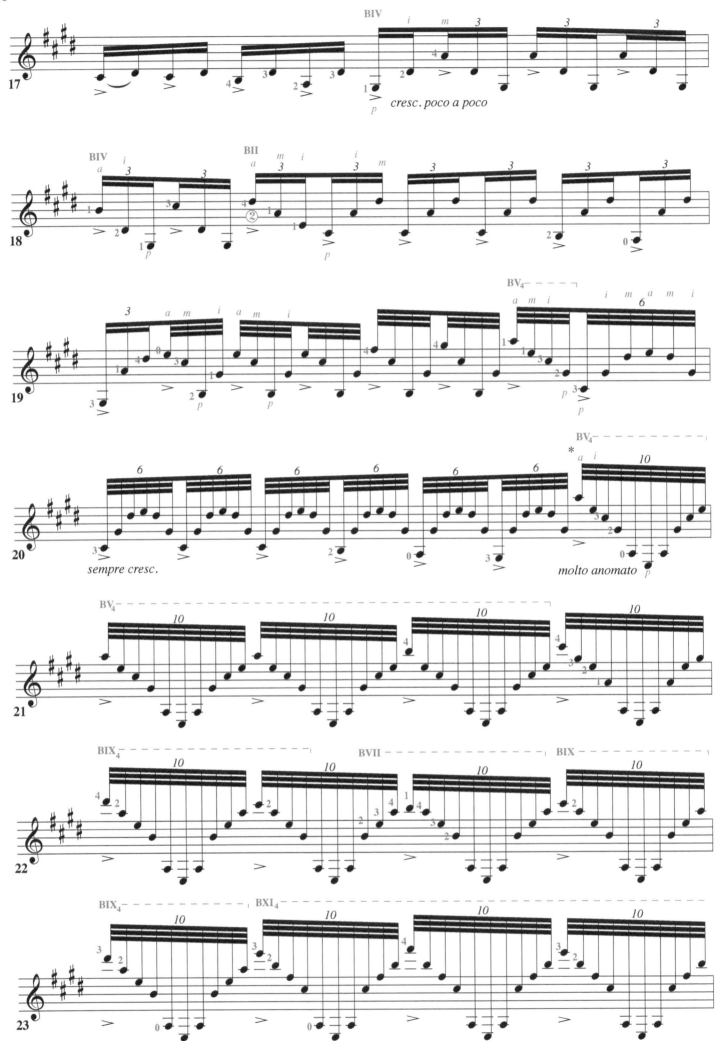

* Refer to ossia on page 265.

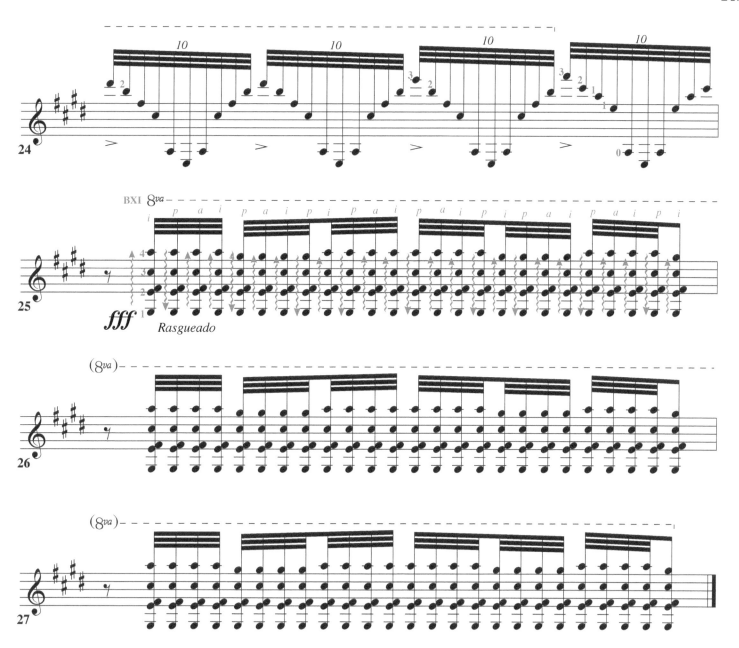

© 1959 Joaquín Rodrigo
Used with the kind permission of Joaquín Rodrigo.

ALSO FROM SCOTT TENNANT

RECUERDOS DE LA ALHAMBRA

by Francisco Tárrega
With Fingerings and Tremolo Instruction

This edition of Tárrega's classic tremolo-based composition "Recuerdos de la Alhambra" includes background information on the composer, detailed tremolo lessons, and thoughtful fingerings from Scott Tennant, one of the world's premier guitar virtuosos. Tennant talks about his own history as a young student learning this piece and shares the method he ultimately developed for mastering the art of the tremolo, a technique that is elusive for many classical guitarists. He provides a progressive set of exercises designed to take you up to a level of familiarity with, and control of, the right-hand patterns one must master in order to develop a smooth tremolo. You'll find two additional version of "Recuerdos de la Alhambra" in this edition—one for the right hand alone, and another in block chords so you can focus on mastering the left-hand connections and shifts required for a musical performance. In one book alone, you have both one of the crown jewels of the guitar repertoire and a way to develop the technique needed to play it. This is a must-have edition for all classical guitarists.

AN ALFRED CLASSICAL GUITAR MASTERWORK EDITION

Classical guitarists, both students and professional performers, require the same high-quality editions that their pianist colleagues have come to expect from Alfred Music. Our Classical Guitar Masterwork Editions continue the Alfred tradition of providing carefully edited, beautifully presented music for practice and performance.

alfred.com